Frome at War
1939–1945

Frome at War
1939–1945

David Lassman

PEN & SWORD
HISTORY

AN IMPRINT OF PEN & SWORD BOOKS LTD.
YORKSHIRE - PHILADELPHIA

First published in Great Britain in 2020 by
Pen & Sword Military
An imprint of
Pen & Sword Books Ltd
Yorkshire – Philadelphia

Copyright © David Lassman, 2020

ISBN 978 1 52670 6 003

The right of David Lassman to be identified as Author of this work
has been asserted by him in accordance with the Copyright, Designs
and Patents Act 1988.

A CIP catalogue record for this book is
available from the British Library.

Printed and bound in England by TJ International, Padstow, Cornwall

Pen & Sword Books Limited incorporates the imprints of Atlas, Archaeology,
Aviation, Discovery, Family History, Fiction, History, Maritime, Military,
Military Classics, Politics, Select, Transport, True Crime, Air World,
Frontline Publishing, Leo Cooper, Remember When, Seaforth Publishing,
The Praetorian Press, Wharncliffe Local History, Wharncliffe Transport,
Wharncliffe True Crime and White Owl.

For a complete list of Pen & Sword titles please contact

PEN & SWORD BOOKS LIMITED
47 Church Street, Barnsley, South Yorkshire, S70 2AS, England
E-mail: enquiries@pen-and-sword.co.uk
Website: www.pen-and-sword.co.uk

Or

PEN AND SWORD BOOKS
1950 Lawrence Rd, Havertown, PA 19083, USA
E-mail: Uspen-and-sword@casematepublishers.com
Website: www.penandswordbooks.com

Contents

Acknowledgements

The gestation of this book, at the time of writing, stretches over almost five years, as I mark the beginning of this journey with my acceptance to organize an event for the Frome Society for Local Studies called 'They Came to Frome'. This was an event for the annual Frome Festival about wartime evacuees who arrived in the town over the first weekend of September 1939 (and later in 1940 and 1944) and stayed either in the town or outlying villages and hamlets such as Mells, Great Elm, Wanstrow, Buckland Dinham and Beckington. Although this event was constrained by its subject matter – in terms of the town's part in the entire war – I had already been commissioned and begun work on the book *Frome in the Great War*, and so it was always my intention I would also write a book on the Second World War and therefore include not only the evacuees which, although important within the story, played a small part in the narrative that became Frome's contribution to the war effort.

If I have missed out anyone from this list then please do know that I consider your contribution no less important than those listed here; it is merely that over this half-decade time frame my memory and notes have, in places, become slightly detached from each other. Those I do remember, however, are as follows: John Payne and Gill Harry and everyone involved with Home in Frome and the *Working Memories* book, along with Brian Marshall, Jon Ryman and others from Frome Museum. Peter Clark for early encouragement and friendship during the lead-up to the evacuee event; George Perry who edited a book of the Coopers Company's School that was evacuated to the town during the war and graciously took part in the evacuee event; Alastair MacLeay and Frome Society for Local

Studies. Mick Davis (and, once again) David Adams' research and resultant book, this time being *Frome's Fallen Heroes of World War Two*; Crysse Morrison, Diane Rouse, Diana Ingram, Martin Easterbrook, Mark Pattison, Michael Mason, Anthony House, Nigel Lassman, Frome Community Education, Frome Writers' Collective and Frome Library; the latter for the fact that they maintain the local newspaper archive on micro-fiche and many a (happy) hour was spent going through the relevant war years. A big thank-you also goes to my wife Claire and our son Michael who, in their own ways, both supported me through the researching and writing of this book.

Also, Roni Wilkinson at Pen & Sword for his initial commissioning of both books – *Frome in the Great War* and *Frome at War 1939–45* – as well as, in no specific order, Matt Jones, Amy Jordan, Heather Williams, Lori Jones and everyone else who has been involved in the process of producing this book.

Finally, to anyone else that has come before me who has undertaken their own research and assembled that resultant information into a readable and/or published format, which ultimately saved me many more hours of labour than the book eventually required. So, like the war itself, this has been a collaborative and combined effort and I thank all those involved.

David Lassman
March 2019

Introduction

Throughout its 1,300-plus-year history, Frome, nestled in the furthest easterly point of the county of Somerset, has always sought to distance itself from involvement in national events, but often finds itself reluctantly drawn into them. On many occasions this has been no more than a supporting role, although at other times more prominent; a defining moment of the West Country Rebellion, for example, happened during the Duke of

Saint Aldhelm, the founder of Frome.

Monmouth's brief stay in the town, while legend has it that a Royal Charter, signed at Frome in AD934, brought into being, for the first time, the notion of England as a unified state.

As for Frome's own existence, this was due to St Aldhelm through his founding of a Saxon church towards the end of the seventh century. A settlement gradually built up around it and by medieval times the town had become an important centre for the woollen industry and cloth trade. So much so that Daniel Defoe wrote that if Frome were to continue to grow at its present rate over the next few years it would most likely become 'one of the greatest and wealthiest inland towns in England'. However, within a century – one that saw the decline of that local industry (in many ways so reflective of the town's story as a whole) – William Cobbett, during one of his 'rural rides', could only record that '[Frome] has received a blow from which it cannot possibly recover.'

Yet recover it did, although not through wool. Other industries, such as printing, metal-working and silk manufacturing, temporarily recovered its prosperity and status, but eventually these too would diminish and Frome would have to find other means to rise itself out of the ashes of depression. Throughout these setbacks, however, the town never shirked its responsibilities within times of national crisis, providing men, monies and munitions towards conflicts from the Napoleonic to the Boer Wars and beyond.

The author's previous book, *Frome in the Great War*, chronicled how the town rose magnificently to the job of 'doing their bit' for the war effort: sending their men (and women) off to the battlefields of France, Flanders and elsewhere, while at the same time making sure they were supported in every way from back home through the sending of parcels to prisoners of war, producing medical supplies for the local hospitals tending the wounded, and digging deep into their pockets for the various fund-raising activities required for the armed forces to defeat Germany and its leader Kaiser Wilhelm II. At the end of it all, when peace came, despite grieving for lost loved ones, the townspeople perhaps took consolation in the fact that they had

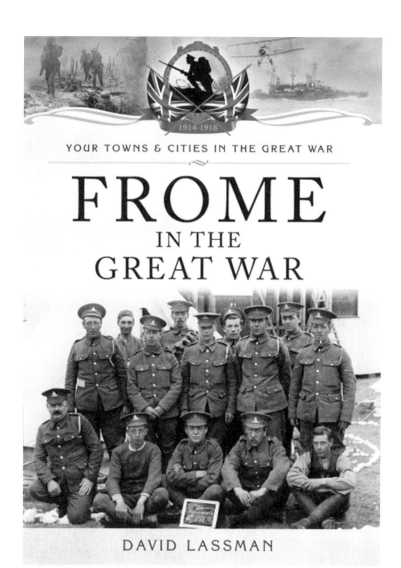

Frome in the Great War (*Pen & Sword, 2016*)

not died in vain, as at least this war meant there would be no future ones.

Just twenty years later, with the Munich Crisis of 1938, it must have seemed to the people of Frome that the lessons supposedly learned from their sacrifice had been forgotten and the town, along with much of Europe, was sliding head-first into another potentially devastating world war. Although this 'crisis' was infamously appeased, it was only a delay and not a resolution to the growing threat of fascism, and in September 1939 the local population and its surrounding areas, along with the rest of the country, found itself once more at war with Germany, now led by Adolf Hitler.

In Frome, this seemingly unbelievable turn of events can perhaps be symbolized by the First World War tank given to the town in gratitude for its financial contribution to the war savings fund. The Mark IV female tank had been presented to Frome in 1919, after being driven from the railway station to its new 'home' in Victoria Park. Like the Versailles Treaty signed that same year, it was meant to be a symbol of the victor's war; at first proudly displayed in the post-war era but slowly, almost unnoticeably, the rust and rot set in and turned it into an eyesore. It is perhaps ironic then that eventually this symbol became

The First World War tank presented to Frome for its financial contribution during that conflict.

such an albatross around the neck of the Frome Urban District Council – as well as a potential death-trap in the eyes of many parents – that in the year of the Munich Crisis it was auctioned off to the highest bidder and sold for scrap.

However, Frome required no symbol from any previous conflict to be galvanized into action for the latest one. Although there was no flag-waving jingoism of the kind that had existed at the outbreak of the First World War, the resolve that had seen the town rise phoenix-like so many times throughout its history remained intact. Not only did Frome once more send its men and women off to the various theatres of war which sprang up all around the globe, but again its people welcomed strangers from around the world – both civilians and uniformed – into their town, their homes and their hearts. Despite this, the Second World War and its immediate aftermath were not

The Market Place in more peaceful times.

without their fair share of controversy including racism, looting, murder and the black market. In many ways, this conflict was vastly different to the previous one, with the influx of American soldiers, the regular sight of aircraft – enemy and Allied – in the skies above, the town and its civilian population becoming a target for the Luftwaffe, the potential threat of poison gas, and

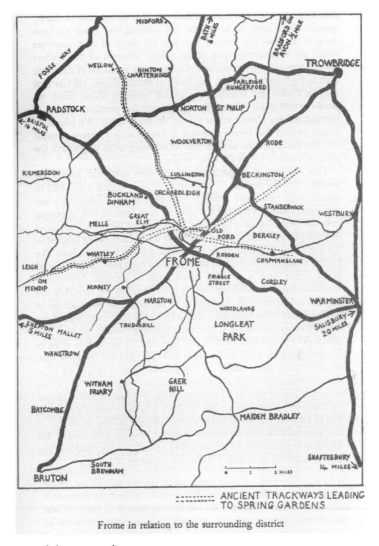

---------- ANCIENT TRACKWAYS LEADING
---------- TO SPRING GARDENS

Frome in relation to the surrounding district

Frome and the surrounding area.

the even greater threat of starvation – if the war in the Atlantic was lost – to name just a few changes.

Here, then, is the story of *Frome at War 1939–45*. For those who lived through it, the author hopes he has done justice to that experience. For those who did not, it is hoped this book will act as a window back into that period of time and also as a permanent memorial to each and every man, woman and child of Frome and the surrounding villages who gave so much during that period in order that we remain free and that this time around, their sacrifice actually ensured that it was the war to end all others on such a massive and destructive scale.

CHAPTER ONE

War Begins: September– December 1939

On Sunday, 3 September 1939 the people of the Somerset market town of Frome found the peace they had enjoyed for the previous twenty years abruptly ended and that they, along with the rest of the country, were once again at war with Germany. The declaration of war had, however, not come out of the blue. Like the First World War, which had ceased those two decades earlier and involved many men and women from Frome, events had been pointing towards conflict during the preceding few years. Since the mid-1930s, the demands and actions of German leader Adolf Hitler had tested the resolve of the British government and although Prime Minister Neville Chamberlain had sought appeasement throughout this period, it was not through personal weakness that he failed, as is often believed, but because he knew the country herself was weak in that she was not yet sufficiently militarily resourced for war. So, in the same manner as the lead-up to the previous hostilities, these pre-war years were used to instigate a programme of rearmament and adequate preparation of defences.

Unlike the First World War, Britain's defence preparations now also had to take into consideration the civilian population on the home front, including those within Frome. The German Zeppelin attacks on several English coastal towns near the end of that former conflict and recent images from the Spanish Civil War had shown how much death and devastation could

Britain's declaration of war is announced.

be inflicted on civilian inhabitants from the air. Indeed, military strategists expected, if war came, that the Germans would launch immediate air strikes that could kill half a million and wound another million people within the first three months of the conflict. So, with this potential threat foremost in their minds, the British government created the Air-Raid Precautions (ARP) Department whose remit was to protect the civil populace from aerial attack, and brought in an official Act compelling all local authorities, including Frome Urban District Council (FUDC) and Frome Rural District Council (FRDC), to create their own ARP services.

By the summer of 1939, as the threat of war continued to hang over Frome and the surrounding villages, its ARP

One of Frome's many ARP squads.

service had become well-established. The county of Somerset was divided into eight areas, each containing its own organizer and staff. Frome was part of No.2 (Bathavon) Area, which included Keynsham, Radstock and Midsomer Norton. Frome's ARP controller was G.H.W. Cruttwell, a well-known solicitor and holder of numerous respected positions within the town, including clerk to the local magistrates. Exactly how efficient the Frome ARP service was, however, would be put to the test during the early hours of Sunday, 9 July 1939. This was the date scheduled for a simulated 'blackout', which would occur during a feigned 'state of emergency' throughout fifteen counties in Southern England, including Somerset. The large-scale exercise was to be held in conjunction with the RAF – who were to carry out night manoeuvres – while Frome's householders and businesses were told to extinguish all lights between the hours of midnight and 4.00 am.

Along with the ARP services, many other aspects of the town's civil defence units were on duty. These included the fire brigade and police – as well as the Auxiliary Fire Service and Special Constabulary – assembled at their respective stations, the First Aid and Rescue parties, together with the Decontamination Squad, all located at Thrasher's Garage at Butts Hill, and the Observer Corps, which operated from their base in the Mary Bailey Playing Fields.

As well as a complete blackout, there were to be twelve staged incidents during the exercise, all taking place in and around the town and designed to test the efficiency of the civil defence forces. The first 'incident' reported to the Civil Defence Centre – based at the YMCA Hall in the High Street – came nine minutes after lights out and involved a high-explosive bomb supposedly having fallen at Fromefield crossroads. Although no casualties were reported, the police were required to divert traffic and inform the military and utilities companies, the latter as both the gas and water mains had been 'destroyed'. Throughout the night, further bombs 'fell', including ones at Wiltshire Buildings, Egford Hill, Cockey's Works, North Parade and Lock's Hill. Along with high-explosive ones, there were several instances of bombs containing poison gas: one near the Post Office in Market Place and others in Weymouth Road and a field behind Vallis Road Cemetery. Meanwhile, an enemy aircraft was reported as coming down in parkland, the scenario being that the pilot had been killed but two unexploded bombs remained on board. The *Somerset Standard* newspaper would later report that although mistakes had occurred in the responses to a number of the incidents, overall, they conceded, 'the trial could be described as completely satisfactory in its endeavour to perfect and unify Frome's A.R.P. organisation.'

A similar exercise took place in August and once again Frome's civil defence services were called on to deal with numerous 'incidents'; this time including two 'major' fires. The first saw a squad of the Frome Fire Brigade called out to the quarry at Castle Hill, Nunney, where a large pile of old tyres and other inflammable material had been set alight, while the

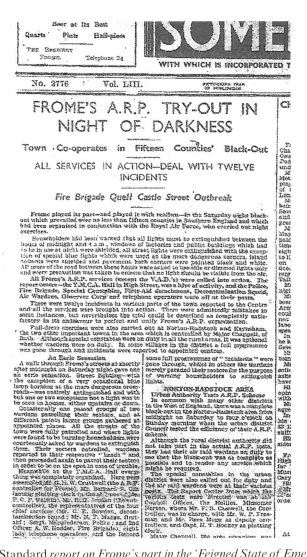

Somerset Standard *report on Frome's part in the 'Feigned State of Emergency'.*

other squad attended Wiltshire Buildings and a blazing derelict property. The Nunney fire was soon put out, but the other, back in Frome, had taken such a hold that it was more than two hours before the fire brigade could bring it under control.

Along with aerial attacks, the possibility of poison gas being used against the civilian population was also a grave worry for the Frome authorities, hence the bomb 'incidents' containing it during the blackout exercises. It had been used against men from Frome on the battlefield in the First World War with dreadful results, but the great fear was that it would now also be unleashed upon the town's civilians. To combat this potential threat, preparations were undertaken to distribute thousands of gas masks throughout Frome and its surrounding areas towards the end of August 1939. 'A Triumph of Organisation', the *Somerset Standard* announced when it reported on the plan's successful execution:

> The assembling and distribution of the gas masks by the local A.R.P. organisation was a triumph of organisation. For more than a fortnight a body of enthusiastic voluntary workers were busily engaged at the depot at Merchant's Barton assembling a huge number of gas masks for distribution over a wide area and by Monday [28 August], the first day on which members of the public could call at appointed centres to fetch them, they had been distributed by motor-van to every village in the Rural area and to all the centres in the town.

These 'town centres' were located at various schools in Frome and included the Council, Christ Church and Holy Trinity schools, St John's Junior School and the Portway Methodist schoolroom. As well as the efficiency that prevailed at the main depot in Merchant's Barton, the newspaper also reported that the centres were apparently so well staffed that 'there were no delays and the majority of masks had been distributed on Monday evening.'

Although Frome men aged between 20 and 22 had been 'called up' to the militia during the summer of 1939, the declaration of war at the beginning of September meant that reservists of other ages across the town received mobilization orders. These were men who were presently serving in the Territorial Army, or else had previously been in the armed forces but had left or retired, with the proviso they could be recalled in the event of war. For Frome's female population, it must have felt like history repeating itself. The majority, no doubt, remembered only too vividly waving off husbands, sons, boyfriends, fiancés, fathers, brothers, uncles, nephews, friends and work colleagues back in August 1914 – many of whom were never to return – and now, a quarter of a century later, they were about to do the same again. This time, though, a completely different atmosphere prevailed in the town. As one letter-writer would record: 'This is a most peculiar war and as different from the 1914 affair as one could possibly imagine. There is no exuberant patriotism, no flag-wagging or cheering crowds, yet every man, woman and child is calm and determined.'

Whereas Frome men had patriotically volunteered in droves at the outbreak of the First World War – responding to Lord Kitchener's famous call to arms – this time the government was taking no chances on being able to elicit such jingoistic fever again, and two days after Poland had been invaded – which had led to Britain declaring war on Germany – parliament passed the National Service (Armed Forces) Act. This meant that all men from Frome and the surrounding villages and hamlets between the ages of 18 and 41, unless already in the forces or a reserved occupation, were now eligible to be called up.

The local newspapers had given quite a few column inches in the previous war to what they termed 'fighting brothers' – several siblings from the same family going off to war together – and this conflict was no different. Examples in Frome included the Taylors – Jim, Ted and Russell – whose parents lived at Mendip View, and the Adlams – Bert, George and Jack – whose father owned a wheelwright business located at Blatchbridge on the outskirts of Frome. Even more incredible were the Chant brothers from Buckland Dinham, as according to the *Somerset Standard*, eight of them ultimately served their country in 'one way or another'. Miraculously, all but one would survive the war and later one of these returning brothers, Fred, would write a book of his reminiscences entitled *It All Seems A Long Time Ago*.

Despite the gathering war clouds during the summer months and the various blackout exercises, the population of Frome and its surrounding villages had attempted to carry on as 'normal'. Probably no example shows this better than the numerous yearly events that took place throughout the region. These included the 12th and 19th Annual Flower Shows at Batcombe and Horningsham respectively, Coleford's 35th Annual Show and the 37th Maiden Bradley and District Horticultural Show, the latter being one of the oldest in the district and which took place 'in weather which was about the same as that experienced by most local shows this season, storms, threatening clouds, and an absence of sunshine which by now has become quite depressing to the organisers of such "summer" functions.' By the August Bank Holiday, however, the weather had broken and although the 17th Annual Fruit, Flower and Vegetable Show, organised by the Corsley Sports, Horticultural and Industrial Society, saw a reduction of entries on the previous year, they nevertheless enjoyed glorious sunshine.

As in the First World War, however, as soon as conflict was certain, shows and events immediately began to suffer. The first casualty was the show organized by the Stratton-on-the-Fosse and Holcombe Horticultural Society, which was cancelled at the 'last minute' on the Saturday before the declaration of war, even though various tents were already set up and amusements had been brought to the location. The Mid-Somerset Agricultural Society Show was also abandoned, despite a grandstand having been erected and the showground prepared at considerable expense. Those that did go ahead – such as the Westfield and Norton Hill Horticultural Society – found entries substantially down due to the 'worsening international situation'. By the following Saturday, once war was declared, the *Somerset Standard* announced that two of the biggest events in Frome's calendar – the Frome Cheese Show and Frome Town Carnival – had been cancelled. The latter event also included the 'Queen of Carnival' competitions and the various Carnival dances arranged in town and villages throughout the area. The newspaper reported that these cancellations at such short notice would mean considerable financial loss to both organizing bodies.

Frome Cheese Show and Carnival Cancelled

DECISIONS WHICH MEAN BIG FINANCIAL LOSS

Both the Frome Cheese Show and the Frome Town Carnival, which were to have been staged in less than a fortnight's time, have both had to be cancelled in view of the outbreak of war.

The decision regarding the Frome Town Carnival was reached at a meeting of the Executive Committee over the week-end. The Carnival was to have been held during the week commencing Monday, Sept. 18th, and the cancellation of the Carnival attractions for the week also includes the Queen of Carnival competitions and all the Carnival dances which had been arranged in town and village.

The necessity of cancellation will mean a serious financial loss to the Carnival, as plans had already been made for the Carnival, and bills and advertisements had already been issued.

The cancellation of the Carnival will also mean a serious loss to the beneficiaries—the Victoria Hospital and the Nursing Association—who every year benefit by a considerable sum.

The Carnival Queen competition had attracted no less than 35 entries, and for the first time it was to have been confined to the Frome Victoria Hospital area.

The Cheese Show

The Committee of the Frome District Agricultural Society, at a meeting on Monday evening, also decided to abandon the 59th annual Cheese Show, which was to have been held on the Fromefield ground on Wednesday, Sept. 20th. Here again plans were well advanced, and the cancellation of the show will involve considerable expenditure.

This year's President of the Society is Mr. Arthur Duckworth, M.P. for Shrewsbury, and son of Major and Mrs. Duckworth, of Orchardleigh House.

Royal Engineers Leave Frome

FOR UNKNOWN DESTINATION

The Frome Field Park Company of the Royal Engineers left Frome early in the week for an unknown destination. A few members of the Company had been mobilised for more than a week, and the remainder of the Company were called up on Friday

Announcement of Cheese Show and Carnival cancellation.

Although the war officially began on the third day of September, Hitler's invasion of Poland two days earlier had triggered not only the National Service (Armed Forces) Act but had also caused several contingency plans to be put into action. One of these was Operation PIED PIPER: the evacuation of children and their teachers – in many cases, entire schools being transferred – from cities deemed vulnerable to German aerial attack, such as London, to places of perceived safety. The British government also included within this operation pre-school children and their mothers or responsible adults, expectant mothers and those adults who were blind or crippled, so far as their removal was feasible. The plan had been conceived in May 1938 by the Home Secretary Sir John Anderson, who would also give his name to the corrugated steel air-raid shelter. It would become the largest mass movement in British history, an exodus dwarfing even the biblical one, according to one newspaper.

Anderson's plan for the evacuation of children and others saw the country divided into three areas: Evacuation, Neutral and Reception. Despite the preparations undertaken by its councils before war started, Frome and its surrounding rural areas were not considered to be at risk and had consequently been placed in the latter category. Throughout the summer of 1939, therefore, families had been sought to become hosts to evacuees in the event of hostilities breaking out. One of these was Muriel Chapman (née Keeping), who at the time lived at 4 Garston Road, Frome. She recalled years later that the authorities 'had come around and asked us. We had no children of our own, so we said yes.' Like other families in Frome and elsewhere, Muriel was to receive 10s 6d a week for taking in an unaccompanied child, or 8s 6d a week for each child when more than one was taken. Where there was a parent or responsible adult with the child, hosts would receive 6s a week for each adult and 3s per week per child. Any householder providing lodgings for teachers or helpers would receive 5s a week.

So successful was the operation to find householders willing to take in evacuated children that by April 1939 the Ministry of Health was able to write:

> In two months' time you, householders of this country [including Frome] have of your own free will enabled us to say that the most difficult part of the evacuation problem, the reception and care of unaccompanied

school children, is solved. I do not know of any nobler or more vital form of National Service that could be undertaken. I should like you to know that we recognise what you have done, and to feel assured that the nation is proud of your ready and sweeping response to this call for service.

This meant that as soon as the British government received news that Germany had crossed the Polish border, the evacuation plan could become operational and on Friday, 1 September 1939 and over the following weekend, trains poured out of London and other cities to rural destinations in the countryside. By the time war was officially declared two days later, more than 1.5 million people had become evacuees.

In Frome, arrangements for the reception of these evacuated children had been undertaken by Frome Urban District Council in collaboration with its counterpart, Frome Rural District Council. 'Frome has always stood up to an emergency,' FUDC Chairman O.L. Seward announced in the *Somerset Standard*, 'and I am sure we can be assured of the wholehearted support of every member of our community.' In total, 3,200 evacuees were expected over four days – Friday to Monday inclusive – with 800 set to arrive on each day. The first train was due at Frome railway station at around 11.40 am on the Friday, as would be the case on each of the other days.

On the first (and second) day of the operation, the parties consisted entirely of schoolchildren from the Shepherd's Bush area of London, including the Coverdale Road Junior Mixed School and Infants, the Ellerslie Road School, and a small party from another school which had inadvertently become detached from their main group. After assembling on the platform and being greeted by specially-created local welcoming committees, all the children were marched down Station Road and marshalled on the high pavement in Portway. They were then escorted, in file and with gas masks around their necks, by billeting officers and other helpers to pre-arranged distribution points – this being either St John's Infants' School or else the Council School (then aka Milk

St School but now known as 'Vallis') – and on arrival there, given a hot meal and refreshments. All children had also been provided with, before they arrived in Frome, emergency rations for the first forty-eight hours which, if not already eaten while on the train, consisted of one can of meat, two cans of milk (one sweetened and one unsweetened), one pound of biscuits and a quarter-pound of chocolate. For adults, such as a mother and child, the allowance was the same except that they received two cans of meat. Children were also given a stamped postcard on their arrival to send back home in order to let their parents know where they had ended up, as the majority of evacuees did not learn of their destination until they arrived at Frome railway station and saw the sign.

Once at the distribution centres, most of the children (and any accompanying adults) were now in the unenviable position of having to be 'chosen' by a host family. Although some family groups were able to stay relatively together, not everyone was so fortunate, as in the example of Pam Lawrence: 'My mother, Norma and myself went to a house in Weymouth Road, staying with a kind elderly couple. My aunty, cousin and brother went off to another family. We really didn't want to be separated, but we had no choice.'

Duly chosen and taken to their host families, the 'shock of the new' often proved to be on both sides. While numerous evacuees had never seen a cow or sheep before, many host families were introduced to certain new types of species as well! Muriel Chapman's experience with her two girl evacuees was relatively typical:

> They looked poor little things there on the doorstep... I thought I must give them a bath and when I stripped them, they were full of flea bites all over their bodies. And when I looked at their hair, they had lice. I had never seen lice before, I must confess, so I popped them in the bath and cut their hair.

On Sunday and Monday of the operation, the trains arriving in Frome also brought with them expectant mothers and younger children, which provoked an editorial in the local newspaper verging on the condescending:

> Pathos and humour went hand-in-hand during the arrival of evacuees at the Frome G.W.R. Station. Most pathetic scenes were provided by the arrival of the mothers and young children on the Sunday and Monday, but although in some cases there were tears at the thought of leaving home everyone was for the most part, very cheerful. House-holders, with very few exceptions, opened their houses to newly-arrived visitors, and a special word of praise is due to the teachers and helpers who assisted with the detraining and billeting.

Like those schoolchildren who had arrived during the previous two days and whose host families were in the surrounding villages and hamlets, a whole cavalcade of vehicles was waiting to transport the arrivals on the final two days. In the latter's case, at least, this consisted of seventy cars and several coaches, all parked up in the station's goods yard.

In the end, only 2,556 evacuees detrained at Frome over the four days rather than the originally expected 3,200, with 1,431 being accommodated in Frome itself and the remaining 1,125 in outlying rural areas. The latter included the village of Mells, which took seventy-seven evacuees over the four days, including schoolchildren and teachers from Oxford Gardens School. Meanwhile, Buckland Dinham received 82 evacuees, Nunney 90, Rode 103 and Beckington 113. Twelve mothers and eighteen children were also welcomed to Orchardleigh House by its residents, Major and Mrs A.C. Duckworth.

The entire operation was deemed a success, with the *Somerset Standard* reporting:

> Frome and district has opened its heart to these refugees from Hitler's bombing planes, and householders everywhere have shown a willingness and a readiness to co-operate in every way. There have been very few

refusals to take evacuees. Altogether the evacuation into Frome, which lasted four days, was expeditiously carried through, and Mr. A.S. Reynolds, who has acted as chief billeting officer for the town and district, is to be congratulated upon the success of his efforts. The scheme was a triumph of organisation and reflected the greatest credit upon everyone.

As well as being a reception area for evacuees, Frome also became a garrison town. During the First World War it had played host to units from the Royal Field Artillery, whose new recruits would undergo twelve weeks of training in Frome before being sent to the front lines. At the outbreak of the latest war, the Frome Field Park Company of the 207th (Wessex) Royal Engineers had been stationed in the town, but left soon after. It was not long, however, before the town was welcoming new military arrivals.

The 5th Battalion of the Dorsetshire Regiment was a Territorial regiment that had seen action during the previous war and already possessed a strong connection with Frome as numerous men from the town had served with the regiment at that time and several had lost their lives in the process. These included Sergeant E. Lloyd, Lance Corporals H. Adams and F. Collier, and Privates W. Button, A. Edwards, W. Oakes and W. Snell. The 5th Dorsets had been disbanded after the armistice but re-formed, under the command of Colonel Sir John Lees, at the beginning of August 1939. Many of the regiment's volunteers were from Poole in Dorset and formed part of 130 Brigade, which itself – along with other 'Wessex'-based regiments, including those from Somerset and Wiltshire – belonged to the 43rd (Wessex) Division. The 5th Dorsets – consisting of around 1,000 men – arrived in Frome not long after the outbreak of war for the purpose of defending it against a possible German invasion, and along with them came the Headquarters staff of 130 Brigade. The sudden arrival of this large number of soldiers requiring accommodation and training facilities obviously made a huge impact on the town, and among the many buildings

D4095/2   PB 2664

NOTICE OF SURRENDER.

To the Owner and Occupier of Land and/or Buildings described in the Schedule hereto annexed.

Notice is hereby given that the War Department will relinquish possession of the Land and/or Buildings described in the attached Schedule as from   25th September 1939.

MAJOR

S.A.Q.C.
"G.L." AREA.

for Command Land Agent,
Southern Command.

SCHEDULE REFERRED TO:-

Buildings and Premises of Curry's Stores, Frome, Somerset.

Notice received of which this is a duplicate.

Owner or Occupier...............................

Date......6. June. 1940......

Compulsory possession of buildings by the government became normal, although not all premises were used in Frome and so several were later relinquished.

GEORGE HOTEL, FROME.

Telephone No. 7.   Garage and Pit.   Proprietor, W. R. BOWN.

The George Hotel in the Market Place.

immediately 'requisitioned' by the incoming force for offices, stores and billets were the George, Portway and White House (later Mendip Lodge) Hotels and Locks Hill House; the White House finding itself chosen as the new HQ for 130 Brigade, while the George Hotel became the officers' mess. One of their first 'duties' on arrival was to be available to help with the harvest:

> 'In view of the vital importance of securing this year's harvest with the least possible delay and of the fact that a number of land workers have recently been called up for military service,' the *Somerset Standard* reported, 'the Ministry of Agriculture has made arrangements with the War Office whereby, subject to operational and

other military requirements, a certain number of serving soldiers will be enabled to give assistance for a few days in the harvest field.'

These arrangements, it was announced, would 'remain in force until 20th September [1939]'.

On top of all these new arrivals – whether civilian or military – there was, of course, the blackout to contend with. When a national newspaper ran a poll a couple of months into the war asking its readers what they hated most about the war, 'the blackout' topped most people's lists. All premises – residential or business – had to have the proper window and door coverings to ensure that not a chink of light emanated from within between half an hour after sunset until half an hour before sunrise. The area's ARP wardens patrolled both town and villages to ensure these regulations were adhered to and those caught breaking the regulations were severely dealt with. Although there were positive aspects to the blackout – the night sky could be seen more clearly without any light pollution, for example, and as cars became more difficult to use, bicycles and horse-drawn traffic multiplied, giving many older residents of Frome and the vicinity a sense of throw-back to an earlier age – for the majority of people, it meant that the possibility of blackout-related accidents rose significantly. Countless pedestrians suffered minor bumps and scrapes sustained from walking into trees in the darkness or tripping off kerbs, while the local newspapers were soon full of reports concerning more serious, and often fatal, incidents; an experience replicated countrywide. In September 1939, for example, the number of people killed in road accidents nationwide doubled, while in the period between October and December, 4,133 people lost their lives compared to only 2,497 in the same period the previous year. The figure for December 1939 alone would be 1,155. These statistics, bad as they were, did not even give the full picture as they excluded those people who crashed through roofs while on fire duty, fell from trains at railway stations or accidentally tripped into canals or rivers.

While the number of motor accidents had risen, the actual number of cars on the road had fallen dramatically and the main mode of transport for people, other than pedal or horse-power, was buses and trains. Austerity buses, as they were known, became a familiar sight, each being able to carry double the numbers of people normally accommodated in a single-decker, and overall the bus companies increased their services throughout the day (although limited them more at night). Rail travel also saw a dramatic increase during the war; within a few years, it would be as much as 70 per cent up on pre-war levels. However, with this increase in demand, trains broke down more often and crowding became almost unbearable during peak times such as Christmas and Easter breaks when families would travel to visit evacuated loved ones or those returning to their own from the front.

In terms of Operation PIED PIPER, Frome's contribution to it was deemed a success; the reception had gone well and for the most part the evacuees had settled in alright. Nevertheless, there were problems that soon became prevalent and had to be dealt with. Perhaps key among them was the hardship caused by staggered school hours. What this meant in practice was that some householders would have to prepare a meal for the evacuee children at 11.30 am and then another for their own children an hour later. Other problems included inadequate bed linen and child allowance payments; the latter certainly not being enough, especially given the double-lunch situation. There were also 'problems' for the evacuees, including lack of books at school and lack of proper bathroom facilities or living space at their new homes:

> 'Farms are particularly difficult,' one report within the Frome Rural District observed, 'frequently several empty bedrooms, but no possibility of separate living rooms, and the busy harassed farmer's wife finds it hard to put up with unoccupied women and children hanging about the place, with habits of behaviour and cleanliness far below her own. The evacuees, too, are despondent over the isolation and sea of mud.'

Along with these teething troubles, the government had the problem of returning mothers; it was reported that by the end of September alone, almost a third had gone back to the capital. The Frome Rural District report also highlighted the dilemmas facing children in their early teens and their mothers:

> The mothers will not, and cannot be expected to, leave them in bombed areas when they bring the younger children to the country, but they object to having to pay for their accommodation. To obtain factory work, such as they are used to, generally entails travelling several miles to the local town, where wages are lower than those received in London and do not cover their board and lodging. Mother is then inclined to take the whole family back for the sake of the older ones' employment.

In light of the situation as it now stood, it seemed a pretty logical choice. The expected air-raids from Hitler had not materialized and in the absence of any foreseeable danger, many undertook the journey back home. By the end of the first month, the exodus had become so bad that the government felt the need to issue posters and the editor of the *Somerset Standard* felt compelled to write the following:

> Despite strong government advice to the contrary, many of the mothers and children evacuated with them from London continue to return home. At least another forty have gone home during the past week, and the total number returned to London since the evacuation started close to five hundred. One wonders whether these returning evacuees will be among the first to ask for re-evacuation in the event of an air-raid on London. Fortunately, among the organised bodies of school children evacuated there have been only one or two children who have returned home. That's not to say that the children who stayed didn't want to return home. Many were homesick, but others found the change to countryside positive.

At the same time as many evacuees were leaving Frome, another several hundred arrived. Although the reception process had gone without a hitch in Frome, elsewhere there had been problems, one of which ultimately had consequences for the town. On Friday, 1 September 1939, along with numerous others in the capital, Coopers' Company's School was given an hour's notice to be ready at Mile End Underground station. From there they were to be taken to Ealing (Broadway) railway station, where a steam train would transport them to their evacuation destination.

The Coopers' Company's School for Boys had begun its existence in 1536, under the title of the Nicholas Gibson Free School. After Gibson's death – a prominent London citizen – his wife asked the Coopers' Company to undertake the school's management and in doing so the name of the school was changed. Situated in Radcliffe on the north side of the River

A Coopers' Company's school class photo with one of the former Army huts used as classrooms in the background.

Thames, the institution merged in 1891 with the Coborn School for Girls, that establishment having also been founded by an individual, one Prisca Coborn.

Now duly boarded on the stream train and en route to their destination, no one on board from the Coopers' Company's School knew where they were headed. Unfortunately, neither did the train driver. They finally arrived at Ramsbury, with the belief that everything had gone as planned. The inhabitants of this small Wiltshire village, however, were not only expecting their evacuees three days later, but also for them to be expectant mothers and babies, not a trainload of East End boys. As it transpired, the school *should* have gone to Taunton – as the Coborn part of the school did successfully – but an administrative mistake somewhere in the process had sent them into Wiltshire, not Somerset.

Determined to make the best of it, however, the school quickly set up classrooms and school rooms within five villages in the area, the school thus being spread over 30 square miles. This situation only lasted for three weeks before it became unworkable. The headmaster was given a choice of three places, including Frome, to which to move the school and after visiting all of them, chose the town. The entire school thus duly packed up once more and boarded another train, which arrived in Frome on 22 September 1939. The site allocated to them was the recently-vacated grounds of Frome Grammar School.

Although the 1902 Education Act had enabled local education authorities to establish county secondary schools and attempts had been made to start one soon after, Frome had to wait almost twenty years before the Frome County Secondary School opened in a group of seven large converted army huts adjoining Northcote House located, as the name would suggest, to the north of the town centre. The 'classrooms' were always seen as a temporary measure, but it was not until almost another twenty years later, in 1939, when the long-awaited permanent buildings were ready and the school moved nearby to the site where the present-day Frome College is situated.

On their arrival in Frome, Coopers' Company's School quickly moved into their new 'home' and, although not ideal for either the children or their teachers, the new arrangements were much better than at Ramsbury in terms of logistics, even if the attitude of the local people they had just left could not be faulted. Lessons began almost immediately, and the school quickly integrated itself within the community. Overall, the school brought around 300 pupils, although this was not their full strength as about 200 boys did not make the trip.

N.R. 50.

 NATIONAL  **REGISTER.**

NATIONAL REGISTRATION DAY IS FRIDAY, 29th SEPTEMBER, 1939.

SEE INSTRUCTIONS IN SCHEDULE AS TO " PERSONS TO BE INCLUDED."

RATIONING.—The return on the schedule herewith will be used not only for National Registration but also for Food Rationing purposes. It is to your interest, therefore, as well as your public duty, to fill up the return carefully, fully and accurately.

Help the Enumerator to collect the schedule promptly by arranging for him to receive it when he calls. Do not make it necessary for him to call a number of times before he can obtain it.

When the Enumerator collects the schedule, he must write and deliver an Identity Card for every person included in the return. Help him to write them properly for you by letting him write at a table.

If the whole household moves before the schedule is collected, take it with you and hand it to the Enumerator calling at your new residence or to the National Registration Office for your new address. The address of this office can be ascertained at a local police station.

Wt 28033—171 12 50

National Registration Day took place on Friday, 29 September 1939.

A week after the Coopers' Company's School arrived in Frome, National Registration Day – Friday, 29 September 1939 – occurred. This had been instigated by the government for the issue of identity cards to eligible citizens and for any future rationing, which they were intent on introducing. Each household was to fill out a schedule to be collected by enumerators. The National Registration Act had been passed at the beginning of September 1939, but with the daunting task of recording the 46 million people that would be affected, it had taken the rest of the month to make the necessary arrangements. Identity cards were issued not long after, and every recipient always had to carry one.

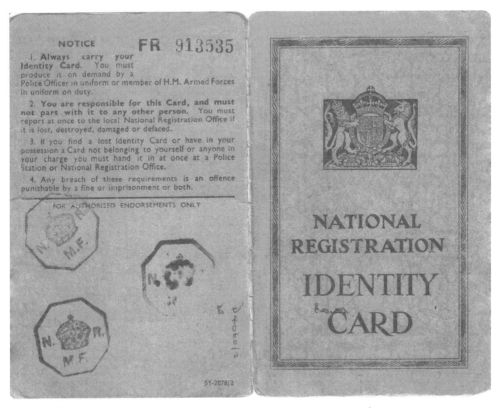

Identity cards were issued in 1939 and always had to be carried.

In October 1939 Frome suffered a major fire that briefly impacted on its contribution to the war effort. Shortly after 11.30 pm on Tuesday, 17 October the town's fire brigade was called out to Merchants' Barton. On their arrival, they found themselves up against what the *Somerset Standard* would label as 'one of the fiercest [fires] experienced in Frome for many years'. The fire was at the Carley Works, in a three-storey building used by the firm of Nott and Beauchamp for manufacturing the famous Carley life-floats and belts. The two upper storeys were completely gutted and everything in them destroyed, including materials, machinery and numerous completed life-floats which were to have been despatched the following morning and ultimately destined for the Admiralty, the Norwegian government and the Mercantile Marine. Less than an hour after the alarm was raised, the building's roof had fallen in and the engulfing flames, rising between 40 and 50ft into the air, could be seen for many miles around.

Nearby residents to the business premises had been first alerted to the fire through a series of loud explosions, which several had initially mistaken for the start of an air-raid. As well as then notifying the emergency services, locals had begun to use a private hose on the fire before the town's brigade arrived. Yet despite this and the three hydrants subsequently being brought into use – ultimately allowing ten jets of water to be aimed at the building from various angles – it took more than two hours for the fire to be brought under control and it was not until dawn before the flames were entirely subdued. By this time, between £8,000 and £10,000 worth of damage had been inflicted and desperately-needed equipment lost. Despite the destruction of its premises though, production of the life-floats recommenced on the following day (Thursday) in another part of Merchants Barton.

Also affected by the fire were the renowned printers Butler and Tanner, who used the basement of the three-storey building as a storeroom. Although the actual flames hardly touched the 100 tons of printed book paper held there by the firm, the estimated 10,000 gallons of water used to extinguish the fire had done untold damage.

The month of October also saw the dismissal of all but one paid ARP worker within the Frome area. They received their 'dismissals' in line with a Home Office order that had arisen as a result of growing criticism over what was seen as the government's excessive spending on paid ARP services nationally and a feeling of discontent among the thousands upon thousands of volunteer wardens and first-aid workers receiving nothing for their services. This decision affected the Report Centre in the High Street – where only the one paid position would remain, so allowing its continuing functionality – the first-aid centres, and all workers manning wardens' posts. In all though, as the *Somerset Standard* was quick to point out in its report on the matter, this equated to the loss of less than a dozen paid positions and not the hundreds it said had been suggested by certain parties. These latter numbers, the paper stated categorically, were 'merely a figment of the imagination'.

By the end of the month the *Somerset Standard*, which incorporated both the *Frome Times* and *Somerset & Wilts Journal* and normally came out on a Friday, reported another reduction of sorts: this time of the newspaper itself. An 'advert' in the 20 October edition announced the decrease in size from that week's issue was due to the urgent necessity of conserving supplies of newsprint; the number of pages going down to four pages, or one sheet of print. However, the price of one and a half pence remained the same, as did its printing works and Newspaper Offices at Stoke House, Christchurch Street West.

As well as children, teachers and accompanying adults, another valuable 'resource' of national importance that needed to be kept safe from possible air attack was the contents of the Public Records Office (PRO) in Chancery Lane, London, so it was decided to move them outside of the capital. Various locations around the country were utilized as secret emergency repositories and these included Belvoir Castle in Leicestershire, Haddon Hall in Derbyshire and Clandon Park, a classical mansion in Surrey. For the most valuable documents and artefacts – which included both the Domesday Book (great and little) and a copy of the Magna Carta – it was decided that the prison at Shepton Mallet in Somerset would be the most secure and ideal place. So when in August 1939 it became almost certain that Britain would go to war, staff at the PRO began the unenviable task of packing up the records into large cardboard boxes and labelling them accordingly, before seeing them loaded into lorries to be transported on their clandestine journey westward to their new home, the original women's wing of the prison. From then on, until the end of November 1939, one, two or even a trio of lorries would leave London daily for Shepton Mallet, passing through Frome in both directions. We know the route included the town because on one of the return journeys from the prison, according to Francis Disney in his authoritative book on the prison, a lorry 'broke down in Frome'. By the end of this mammoth undertaking, nearly 10,000 large cardboard boxes had been transported.

Shepton Mallet Prison.

It had been strongly rumoured that the Crown Jewels were also relocated to Shepton Mallet prison as part of this 'Secret Hoard', but in his book, Disney states he had yet to find any physical proof to substantiate the claim and then reprints the official statement on this matter taken from the Constable's Office at the Tower of London, which reads: 'The Crown Jewels were removed from the Tower of London to a place of safety during the [Second World] war. The location was secret and no written records were kept. I have heard many rumours but can confirm or deny none.' With this level of mystery and intrigue, it is not surprising that many other places in the decades since the war lay claim to have been the secret location, which also included a secured basement room at Sexey's Hospital in Bruton. The truth, as we now know through a recent revelation, is that this 'place of safety' was inside a biscuit tin buried deep inside Windsor Castle!

If the First World War had begun in August 1914 with the feeling that it would all be over by Christmas, there were likely to be few people in Frome who believed it this time around. Nevertheless, and 'Despite the war clouds,' according to a report in the *Somerset Standard*, 'Christmas in Frome was celebrated in the customary manner. In the institutions Christmas fare was provided in ample quantities and every effort was made to make the festive season an enjoyable one.' Elsewhere, the town's first Christmas of the war also seemed to proceed as normally as could be expected, although obviously within the tight regulations of the blackout and the absence of so many loved ones. There were certain surreal aspects to the festive period though, as shops in the town were only allowed to light their window displays early in the morning as people were on their way to work, night displays being strictly forbidden due to the blackout. The Post Office, meanwhile, anticipating a huge surge in demand for their services across the festive period, advertised not only for temporary staff but also for early posting of parcels, letters and cards. Their forethought was well-placed, as the total of incoming and outgoing parcels and Christmas cards easily exceeded the numbers of previous years and harked back to the festive periods of the previous war.

With 1939 at an end, the people of Frome could only imagine what the coming year and those that followed it might bring, and if they did not believe it would be a short war, they had little way of knowing that this was to be the first of what would be six wartime Christmases and New Years that ultimately occurred before the Second World War was over.

CHAPTER TWO

The Waiting is Over: January–June 1940

For the population of Frome, as elsewhere, 1940 began badly. Firstly, the winter would turn out to be the coldest for forty-five years and, as the *Somerset Standard* would report at the month's end, 'January 1940 will go down in history as a month in which some of the worst weather within living memory was experienced in all parts of the country.' Although there had been occasions when the snow was deeper, the newspaper announced, never had conditions of ice and snow been experienced with such severity and for so long a period; even the oldest inhabitants of the town could not remember anything quite like it.

The extreme weather arrived during the first week of January and within a fortnight was so cold that the River Thames froze for the first time in more than fifty years. In Frome, the lakes at Orchardleigh and Sherwater also iced over, allowing locals and schoolchildren alike to enjoy some unexpected winter activities. Elsewhere in the town, milk froze solid on doorsteps and coal supplies ran out. Many roads in and out of Frome became impassable and, nearer the centre, Bath Street also became like an ice rink, albeit one with a very steep slope. Numerous pedestrians incurred broken limbs from falls, and later in the month several schools were forced to close for at least a week and public transport and railway timetables became almost redundant. Pipes, railway signals, points and water systems froze solid, while telegraph poles were snapped off like broomsticks.

The lake at Orchardleigh became a skating rink in the winter of 1940.

Throughout Frome and the surrounding districts, although more acutely in the heavily-forested areas, there was considerable damage to trees, with branches and twigs strewn everywhere, including on the major roads:

'The strangest sight of all,' reported the *Somerset Standard*, 'was to see rain descending out of the heavens and rapidly freezing on every branch and twig and blade of grass until they became several times their normal thickness. Blades of grass encased in ice which stood up like bristles presented an intriguing picture, and despite the discomforts and disadvantages one could not help but admire the beauty and picturesqueness of the landscape held in Jack Frost's nippiest grip.'

The weather, however, only added to the miserable start. On the first day of 1940 more men from Frome, this time between

Ration books became ubiquitous from January 1940.

the ages of 19 and 27, found themselves called up. They were among the 2 million men nationwide who received their papers at this time. Also, not long after the bad weather had begun, food rationing finally became a reality. There had been attempts to introduce it earlier – within the preceding two months – but on both occasions it was postponed as a fearful government was concerned about the public's reaction. So, on 8 January

1940, it became a way of life for the town's population, and incredibly rationing would not be totally lifted until eight years after the war itself had ended. The first items to be rationed were butter, sugar, bacon and ham, followed a couple of months later by other meats and at a later date by cheese and additional foodstuffs. It was cheese, along with meat, that would cause the most complaints regarding rationing in the town. To add further confusion and misery to the mix, allowances for various items would fluctuate throughout the war. There was no aspect of ordinary civilian life that was not affected by rationing as clothing and petrol, among other everyday items, would come under strict regulations.

As the first months of 1940 wore on, there was still no major activity on land or in the air in terms of the war and several names were coined for this time of inaction. The 'Bore' (paraphrasing the Boer War that had taken place at the beginning of the century) and 'Twilight' were two of them, but most people would come to know this period as the 'Phoney War'. The truth, however, as the majority of people knew, was that given the extreme cold, it would not be until spring and the advent of more clement weather that Hitler would make any move on land. When it did finally come, it would change the nature of land warfare forever.

There had, of course, been continuing hostile confrontations and resultant casualties since the start of the war back in September 1939, but these had taken place mainly at sea within what became known as the Battle of the Atlantic. With Britain reliant on materials for war production and food to feed her population coming from abroad, this made her vulnerable to a German naval blockade. If the British Merchant Navy was unable to deliver the all-important supplies, there was every possibility that the country might be starved into surrender, hence the perceived need by the British government to ration those resources already held. At the start of the war, however, Britain possessed the largest merchant fleet in the world and along with the 4,000 vessels that it comprised, 200 Royal Navy vessels were assigned to protect them from the enemy. Having

U-boats posed the biggest threat to Allied convoys bringing urgently needed supplies.

learned their lesson from the painful experiences of the First World War, the convoy system was introduced almost as soon as war had broken out.

There were several ways in which the German navy attempted to impose this 'blockade' and stop these convoys getting through – surface raiders such as battleships and cruisers, mines and aerial bombers among them – but by far the greatest threat to Allied shipping and the one that inflicted the heaviest loss of life and tonnage was the German U-boat. Although the submarine's full potential had not been truly realized by either side prior to 1939, the U-boat's ability to cause large-scale destruction once the war had begun, either through acting alone or as part of a 'wolf-pack' strategy, became one of extreme concern; so much so that Churchill himself would later state that 'the only thing that really frightened me during the war was the U-boat peril.'

Almost from the outset of the war, the Royal Navy experienced a number of high-profile naval losses, with the sinking of HMS *Courageous* and *Royal Oak* probably the most notable. Thankfully, however, there had not been any reported fatalities from Frome or the immediate vicinity (although several men from Bath had gone down with both ships, along with others from just outside the Frome area, such as Dilton Marsh and Codford). That is not to say that the town had no connection with these incidents. For example, Petty Officer E.A. Rowland, nephew of the rector in nearby Wanstrow, was reported as a survivor of HMS *Royal Oak*, while another survivor from that ship, Second Lieutenant Anthony H. Pearman, RNVR, had been, according to the *Somerset Standard*, a member of the Henleaze Swimming Club that had visited pre-war Frome to compete on several occasions.

There was an actual native of Frome listed as a survivor on another ship that had been sunk by a German submarine, but this time it was a commercial vessel. On the day after the declaration of war, out in the Atlantic, the SS *Athenia* was torpedoed by a U-boat. The ship was a transatlantic liner owned by the Donaldson Atlantic Line. She had left Glasgow three days earlier to sail to Montreal in Canada, and had stopped at Liverpool and Belfast. The ship was a couple of hundred nautical miles north-west of Ireland when she was sunk with the loss of more than 100 passengers and crew. The sinking was contrary to all codes of international law and the incident had profoundly shocked the world. At the time Germany denied responsibility, but some time after the war was over finally admitted to the sinking, although even then the U-boat captain claimed he had mistaken the liner for an armed merchant cruiser. One of the survivors, however, was Mrs E. Mitchelmore, who originally came from Frome. Although apparently born in the town, she had lived for a time in Bath before having emigrated to Canada. She had been back in this country on holiday at the outbreak of the war, staying at her sister's in Combe Park, Bath, and had boarded the *Athenia* in Liverpool to return to her adopted 'homeland'.

Another incident that generated international headlines but had a connection with the town was the demise of the German battleship *Admiral Graf Spee* back in December. This was during the Battle of the River Plate – the first major naval engagement of the war – in the South Atlantic off the coast of neutral Uruguay. The initial clash was between the *Graf Spee* and

HMS Exeter.

three British ships, HMS *Exeter*, *Ajax* and *Achilles*. Although *Exeter* was severely crippled, the accompanying cruisers, along with the German battleship, incurred only moderate damage. However, in the case of the latter this proved critical as it was the fuel system that was hit. Taking refuge in the port of Montevideo, the Uruguayan capital, the German captain ultimately scuttled his ship.

Aboard HMS *Exeter* and one of her survivors, as the *Somerset Standard* would later report, was Stoker 1st Class Frederick Oliver of 14 Long Ground, Frome. He had joined the navy five years earlier and had been drafted to the *Exeter* two years into his service. After news of his participation in the battle became known, Frome Urban District Council, at their monthly meeting, decided to recognize his actions. As the stoker 'was the only member of the crews of the three British ships which took part in the engagement to come from Frome,' said the chairman, when he brought up the matter, '[he] felt sure that the council would like to do something to commemorate the occasion'. The chairman then asked Mr Russ, as a representative of the British Legion, to move a proposal, which he did with the following: 'Stoker Oliver's participation in the battle should be recorded in the minutes and that they [the FUDC] should send him a letter of appreciation and best wishes, he being the only representative of the town in that particular naval battle.' Mr Russ added that he understood 'that this young man has been in the Navy for some five years and previous to joining he was a member of the Rugby Club and also, I believe, of the Swimming Club'. After the proposal was seconded and unanimously carried, the chairman also proposed that a letter of congratulation be written to Mrs Oliver on having such a husband [the couple having married only the previous Sunday at the Frome Registry Office]. Sadly, this story has a tragic ending. Although receiving the appreciation of his home town council and later being promoted to Petty Officer Stoker, Frederick Oliver was killed in action on 16 June 1942 while serving aboard a new ship – HMS *Hermione* – which was sunk by a German U-boat during convoy duties.

Although there had been no fatalities of men from Frome due to enemy action in 1939, there had been two deaths. Both had occurred in November of that year and while one was a tragic accident, the other was through illness.

In the early evening of 24 November 1939, Donald Reginald Adams, a gunner with the Royal Artillery, was waiting for a bus outside his camp with several comrades when he was knocked down by a motor van, dying in hospital from his injuries the next day. The 20-year-old was the eldest son of Mr and Mrs A.E. Adams of 7 Robins Lane, Frome and had only been called up eight weeks prior to his death. He had been a pupil at St John's Senior School and on leaving had been first employed by the Frome Co-operative Society and then latterly, before his recent call-up, in the bottling department of the Lamb Brewery in Frome. On being conscripted into the Royal Artillery, Gunner Adams had been stationed at Norton Manor Camp in Taunton, outside of which he had sustained his fatal injuries.

The inquest into his death, held on the following Tuesday, exonerated the van driver, Mr Bertie Burrows. According to the testimony given, Donald and between twenty-five and thirty fellow soldiers were lined up on the other side of the road to the camp entrance waiting for a bus when knocked down. They had begun waiting at around 5.15 pm and by then it was already dark. Burrows, the driver, said in a statement:

> About 5.30pm I was passing the Camp and I had two side-lights on and the offside head-lamp. I know there is generally a crowd of soldiers stood outside the entrance to the Camp and I have at various times when passing picked up soldiers, and as I got to the entrance of the Camp I slackened speed to ten to twelve miles an hour. I do not think there was any vehicle or person coming towards me. As I was passing the entrance I heard a shout and I pulled up my van suddenly. I was close in to my proper side when I heard the shout. I got out of the van. I did not feel any bump and stopped for the purpose of giving the soldier who I thought shouted a lift. Then several soldiers ran around my van and said there was a man underneath the van.

On giving his evidence, Dr Godfrey Carter, the pathologist at the hospital where Adams was taken after the accident and where he had subsequently died, said the cause of death was haemorrhage upon the brain due to a fractured skull. A verdict of accidental death was recorded, and the coroner, expressing sympathy for the deceased's relatives, said that Adams had died on active service just as much as any soldier in France. His funeral took place the following Saturday at the Holy Trinity Church in Frome.

The other fatality in November 1939 also died from a non-combatant cause, namely bronchial pneumonia. Thomas Ernest Carpenter was a 50-year-old Stoker Petty Officer, who lived at 3 Caxton Road, Frome. Thomas, a native of the town, had joined the Royal Navy in 1910 and had served through the Great War and afterwards, spending his first eight years of service in submarines and the remaining seven and a half years in other

Christchurch, which is the location for several war graves from both world wars.

ships. Apparently the underwater vessels on which he saw duty were the infamous K-class submarines, which went from drawing board to active service without any trials. Subsequently, not a single K-class submarine escaped a serious accident, resulting in appalling loss of life.

Thomas Carpenter, however, survived not only the K-class submarine debacle but the Great War itself, and on leaving the navy a few years later, went to work for Butler and Tanner, an employment he held until recalled to the navy the previous August. He was by all accounts a very popular person in the town, not least as he was a member of several clubs and organizations, held several official positions in many of them and, along with his wife, had been in charge of the Butler & Tanner canteen at Adderwell Works for ten years. Once back at sea, he had seen service with the North Sea contraband control, before being stricken by pneumonia. He had been taken to the Haslar Naval Hospital in Gosport, where he passed away on 28 November 1939.

The first four months of 1940 saw no further casualties, either through enemy action or for non-combatant reasons, but this would change dramatically in May 1940. Throughout that month and the previous one, Hitler had finally made his move, and in a short period of time several western European countries found themselves under German rule. Denmark and Norway were first in April, swiftly followed by Belgium and Holland in early May. The speed with which the Germans had been able to conquer their neighbours was mainly due to the fact that their highly-motorized war machine was able to move at lightning speeds, leading to the term 'lightning war' or 'Blitzkrieg', and throughout the spring of 1940, with nothing seemingly able to stop its interminable momentum, made its way towards France; bringing to an end not only the 'Phoney War' but a whole tradition of how wars were fought.

Like their predecessors in the First World War, the British Expeditionary Force (BEF) had arrived in France with high hopes but, just as before, any early success was swiftly wiped out by retreat, defeat and high casualty rates. This time, the BEF was part of the resources commanded by the French commander-in-chief General Gamelin. His plan was simple. When (rather than if) a German attack came, the imposing French defensive Maginot Line would more than likely divert it through Belgium. Gamelin would then rush his best troops, including the BEF, towards that area, where they would hold back the Germans along the River Dyle in Belgium. On 11 May 1940, the day after Hitler put his planned invasion of the Low Countries into action, the BEF duly arrived at its intended position along the riverbank. In the end though, the Allied defenders were outsmarted and outmanoeuvred, with the main thrust of the German attack being centred further south. Once again, the speed with which it was executed took everyone by surprise.

Three days later, however, on 14 May 1940, a German force did appear on the opposite bank of the Dyle and fierce fighting began. In 1918, the BEF had consisted of the best fighting machine in the world, but during the interwar period, defence cuts had pared it back to a point where the majority of its troops, although abounding in enthusiasm, lacked experience. On 17 May, the BEF withdrew and by the next night met up with its reserve force dug in along the River Escaut, deeper into Belgium. From here, the leader of the BEF, Lord Gort, ordered a counter-attack near Arras. After initial success, the momentum stalled and they again withdrew, this time to the Franco-Belgian border, arriving there on 22 May. The following day, Gort ordered his troops to draw back towards the French port of Dunkirk, a decision that ultimately saved the BEF from complete annihilation.

From the start of Germany's expansion into the Low Countries, the number of men from the Frome area killed in action began to rise significantly. On 18 May, George Thomas William Blackwell, lieutenant (quartermaster) of the 7th Battalion, Royal Sussex Regiment, which formed part of the BEF, was killed in action. His wife Grace was the daughter of Mrs J.G. Brimble, who lived at 9 Sheppard's Barton, and they had one child, a girl. Lieutenant Blackwell had been recalled to active service at the outbreak of war, having previously served twenty-one years in postings such as Singapore. He is buried at the Abbeville Communal Cemetery Extension, Somme, in France. So, to all intents and purposes, he became the first man from Frome to be killed by enemy action.

Five days later, on the 23rd of the month, Leonard John Anstey was also killed, as the 21-year-old second lieutenant in the 1st Battalion, Royal Berkshire Regiment defended the Scheldt line in Belgium against invading German forces. Although born in Sparkford near Yeovil, the Anstey family had moved to Rudge Hill Farm (now Rudge Manor) near Standerwick, Frome in 1920. Leonard had attended Frome County School (aka the Grammar School and now Frome College) for seven years – where he is one of fourteen 'old boys' remembered on their Memorial Plaque – after which he won a United Dairies scholarship and went to Reading University. After obtaining his BSc in Agriculture, he was called up to the militia and had been in the army for nearly a year before his untimely death. He is

Frome College plaque commemorating the fourteen 'old boys' who died in the Second World War.

buried at Chercq Churchyard, Belgium, along with many of his comrades who died in the same action.

On the same day that Lieutenant Anstey was killed in Belgium, back across the Channel, on the Wiltshire Downs, another life with a local connection was lost in another tragic accident. Frederick J.C. Dunn of Beechwood Avenue, Frome, a lance corporal with the 207th Field Park Company Royal Engineers (who had previously been stationed in the town) was in charge of a patrol out on the Wyle Downs. After ordering a comrade to load his rifle, on spotting what Dunn believed to be movement in a small copse, the weapon went off and shot the lance corporal in the stomach. The verdict on the incident at the subsequent inquest was one of 'accidental death'. Before the war, Frederick Dunn was employed at Butler & Tanner as an offset printer but had been called up with the Territorial unit at the outbreak of war. He had been a prominent sportsman within the town, being a member of the Frome swimming and rugby clubs. He was buried in his home town of Guildford, with full military honours. He was 26 years old and left a widow and one small child.

Operation DYNAMO, the evacuation of the BEF from Dunkirk, took place between 26 May and 4 June 1940. Although in military terms it was a complete disaster – equipment, ammunition and transport were abandoned, countless men lost their lives, and the main objective of the BEF being sent over to France had failed miserably – it nevertheless quickly attained mythic status in the eyes of the British public. There is certainly something to be said about the events that unfolded during those few days and nights in the late spring of 1940, when a small armada of marine craft of all shapes, sizes and descriptions – naval, merchant, civilian and private – made their way across the English Channel, time and time again and under heavy fire, to ultimately rescue more than 338,000 British and French soldiers from the clutches of the approaching German army.

Men from Frome and the surrounding districts were on both sides of the operation, so to speak, as both rescuers and rescued. Not everyone from the BEF who made it to the Dunkirk coast managed to be evacuated off though: many died on the beaches or were simply not seen again once the rescue crafts had left. One of the former was Lieutenant John Cuncliffe Shawe, who died four days before Operation DYNAMO officially commenced. The 23-year-old Lieutenant Shawe of the 16th Field Regiment, Royal Artillery had been a career soldier and the son of Lieutenant Colonel Charles Shawe CBE of 'The Hermitage', Witham Friary, near Frome. He had gone across to France as an original member of the BEF back in 1939, and is buried in Dunkirk Town Cemetery.

For those successfully brought back to England, however, it was not all plain sailing as in many cases tragedy was waiting. Perhaps one of the saddest stories of those that did return was of Lance Corporal Harry Sweet. The military policeman and recent evacuee with the BEF from Dunkirk was travelling to visit his wife, who was staying with a sister in the Odd Down area of nearby Bath. As he made his way through Frome, Lance Corporal Sweet was accidentally crushed by a bus in the centre of town. He was taken to Bath's Royal United Hospital, but subsequently died of his injuries. An inquest held the following Wednesday returned a verdict of 'Accidental Death'.

Throughout the first part of June 1940, Frome experienced what Reverend W.J. Torrance, the vicar of Frome, later described in a letter to one of his successors as 'the arrival of great numbers of evacuees from Dunkirk who trooped down Vicarage Street from the station in an unending stream'. The parish hall, however, quickly became an emergency canteen for the soldiers on their way to Market Place [the parish hall would later become a more permanent canteen and recreation centre for those troops who remained stationed in the town]. Once in the centre of town where an elaborate distribution centre had been set up, the soldiers' appearance would be long remembered by those who witnessed the heartbreaking sight:

> A group of us Coopers' [Company's School] boys were on the bridge over the river in Frome when a platoon of soldiers who had just come back from France came marching along. They look tired and weary; their uniforms were dirty and they were obviously from different regiments. As they came over the river bridge they threw their rifles into the river! They were just so tired and fed up with war!

Although these schoolboys could only stand and watch the soldiers' despair, others tried to alleviate it, as another schoolboy, Ron White, remembered in the book *Working Memories*:

> [In] This whole area in front of the new library [in what is also today part of the Cheese & Grain car park] there were hundreds of soldiers that came back from Dunkirk with no shoes, boots, no shirts, terrible state, and all the women of Frome were giving them tea, putting blankets round them. [At the same time, the FUDC voted unanimously to allow the men the use of Victoria Swimming Baths free of charge for the duration of their stay in the town.] My father used to drive for Roads Reconstruction during the war, and he went off for three or four weeks at least, maybe longer, transporting all these [returning] soldiers...

In 1940 soldiers returning from Dunkirk were given refreshments and comforts here.

from the coast [to reception camps throughout Britain, from Aldershot to Lancashire, from Wales to Yorkshire, regardless of the units to which they belonged].

Despite their dilapidated and exhausted state, there was still courage in the soldiers and this was shown by an incident that occurred, which again was witnessed by Ron, who was 6 years old at the time:

There was one chap sat on the floor with a blanket over him, and opposite, where the little footbridge is now, the ground used to come down to river level there, and there was a young girl with a baby in a pram on the other bank watching what was going on. She must have let go of the pram and it careered down the bank and straight into the river, with the baby in it. And one of these chaps jumped up, threw his blanket off, and he dived in. There

The Victoria swimming baths.

was a very high bank this side with all brambles and he
dived right over the bushes and into the water, took a
hell of a chance because there were places where it was
very shallow, and got this baby out. And he'd just come
back from Dunkirk!

As well as the presence of continued courage, love actually found
a way to blossom between the dishevelled and those tending
them, as another 'memory' recounted in *Working Memories* by
the group Home in Frome reveals. John Fairhurst was a regular
in the Royal Artillery, remembered Winifred Fairhurst, who was
one of the women helping the soldiers, but

[w]hen they came back from Dunkirk, some of them
never had no boots on or anything. They were all dirty
and wet. And they came through and we gave them cups
of tea. Then they went [to one of the reception centres]
and got sorted out and then they came back to Frome.
I met John at a dance in the Keyford Drill Hall and we
got married in 1942. He was a Wigan boy.

The Drill Hall at Keyford, which was opened in February 1914.

The reason John and his comrades from the Royal Artillery 'came back to Frome' was that three regiments of the Royal Artillery – the 7th, 33rd and 76th Highland – to one of which John belonged, were part of the 3rd (Iron) Infantry Division, whose divisional HQ had now been relocated to a small hotel within the town.

While in France, as part of the BEF, the 3rd Division had been commanded by the man who, after Churchill, would come to symbolize, at least in Britain, victory in the Second World War and become the most celebrated war hero since Horatio Nelson: Field Marshal Bernard Montgomery. In 1940, while in charge of the 3rd Division, however, he was still a major general, and the great victories on which his everlasting reputation would be founded lay in the future. At this time, his main concern was for the fitness of his men and the need to rehearse for retreat in what he now saw as a losing battle in France.

Bernard Law Montgomery was born on 17 November 1887 in Kennington, Surrey, but before the age of 2 his family moved to Tasmania and he would not return to England until he was 13. Once back, he attended the Royal Military College at Sandhurst and later fought in the First World War, including the Battles of Arras and Passchendaele. At the outbreak of the Second World War he had been a major general for about a year, having commanded the 8th Infantry Division in Palestine. He had returned once more to Britain, in July 1939, to take command of the 3rd Division.

Montgomery's forethought paid off when, after the Germans' overwhelming advance, the 3rd Division withdrew

At the time Montgomery stayed in Frome he was still a general.

to Dunkirk with great professionalism, entering the area's perimeter in a famous night-time march that placed his forces on the left flank which had been left exposed by the Belgian surrender. Although not yet in the very top echelons of command, Montgomery nevertheless made his views known, which ruffled the feathers of many of his military peers and even a few superiors, but the men under his command came to adore him and would do anything for him. At the same time, his military prowess and skills during the Battle of France were already being recognized and appreciated in certain quarters and before the 3rd Division left France, he was promoted to commander-in-chief of the 2nd Corps. On the eve of his departure as their head, he wrote a Special Order of the Day to his men, which included John Fairhurst:

> We have been through much together since mobilization last September, and I had hoped to be able to lead the 3rd Division safely through the present difficulties. But one has to do one's duty and I have now to take over command of the Corps; the 3rd Division is in the 2nd Corps and I shall make it my special task to watch over its welfare. I have asked that on return to England I may be allowed to return to the 3rd Division if I am no longer required as a Corps Commander.... We have not quite finished our task yet, and the next two or three days may see some hard fighting. Provided we maintain our present positions, all will be well...[and] during the next few days we shall need stout hearts and cool heads, and all must be prepared to uphold the good name of the 3rd Division by hard fighting.

As history records, Operation DYNAMO – the evacuation of the BEF back to Britain – saw more than 300,000 soldiers safely returned, but even as the men were drinking their well-earned cups of tea in Frome, plans were being made to send many of them back across the Channel to carry on the fight. Winston Churchill, who by now had succeeded Chamberlain as prime minister, later wrote in his book *The Second World War*, regarding the aftermath of Dunkirk, that 'First priority continued to be given to sending whatever trained and equipped troops we had in order to reconstitute the B.E.F. in France.' In the end, it was decided that there were only enough resources for a single division to be re-equipped and sent back to France and this turned out to be the 3rd, who had returned to Britain virtually intact – sans equipment – with minimal casualties. It was also agreed that Montgomery could return to command them. So, after Frome had been chosen as the location for the new divisional HQ, Major General Montgomery travelled to the town, arriving on 6 June 1940.

The Portway Hotel had been chosen as divisional HQ during Montgomery's stay, having recently been vacated by the 5th Dorsetshire Regiment, which had been stationed in the town since the previous September. No. 20 Portway had been built originally as a private house around 1800, but had been converted into a hotel, complete with licensed bar, in 1934, five years before being requisitioned by the War Office.

The Portway Hotel in Frome which Montgomery used as his headquarters in June 1940.

Despite the loyalty of the men of the 3rd Division towards Montgomery, their renewed acquaintance in Frome did not get off to the best of beginnings. This was due to the fact that Montgomery decided there would be no leave for any of the men to see their families before their return to France. Although he went round personally to inform his men – now billeted throughout East Somerset and beyond – of the reasons behind his decision, the news was received extremely badly. In fact, men of one regiment, the Coldstream Guards, temporarily stationed in Radstock, even barracked him!

His ability as a leader of men, however, showed itself on his return to his Portway HQ as one of the men under his command would be quoted as saying in the authorized biography on Montgomery by Nigel Hamilton:

> He came back to his HQ in Frome that evening. He sent for his chief of staff and his head of Divisional administration and asked the latter about the likely schedule for re-equipment. The head of administration said the tap had been turned on, but that the stuff wouldn't come in for another 48 hours by the time it was unloaded, checked, etc. After considerable discussion Montgomery suddenly said: 'Right, everyone in the Division must go on leave for 48 hours from tonight!' We were stunned. It meant that he was completely reversing the command he had given verbally to practically every officer, NCO and soldier in the Division that day. The order was sent out immediately – it was already between 7 and 8pm. 'There we are,' he explained to his commanders, 'supplies are not coming through as quickly as we thought. Therefore you must all go on 48 hours' leave from midnight tonight!' He got a very high feeling of admiration from the Division for being able to reverse his own decision like that. It showed his stature, the realism that underlay his absolute professionalism. The Division dispersed overnight; the supplies came through; and with fresh determination we prepared to go back to France.

While his men were on leave, Montgomery set about considering every aspect of the war, from billets and training to grants and plans for the return to France; all of which were discussed and considered in even more detail with his officers in almost daily meetings once they returned. In addition to this, he ordered them to provide him with their written views on lessons learned during the Dunkirk campaign and later in his short stay, he issued a five-page memorandum entitled: 'Important lessons from the operation of the BEF in France and Belgium May 1940', together with twenty-two pages of appendices (in which he was the first to acknowledge the superiority of German tactics). Montgomery was already famous for

> the iron discipline which now ruled his personal life – his abstinence from drink or tobacco, his rigid mealtimes, his ordinance about regular sleep [and] the record of his work in the 3rd Division after his return from Dunkirk is phenomenal, and demonstrates clearly Bernard was driving himself harder than anyone.

Montgomery was not the only one working himself 'phenomenally' hard, as so too were many local Frome people, especially those who belonged to the Women's Voluntary Service. The WVS, as it was originally called – it would later be allowed to add 'Royal' to its title – was started by Lady Stella Reading in the spring of 1938 and was created in order to work in association with the Home Office, local authorities and ARP. In Frome, the WVS had already been very active since the start of the war. They had distributed gas masks in August 1939; received and billeted the evacuees who arrived in numbers the following month – as well as sorting out any subsequent problems that arose – and had begun all manner of initiatives, including a clothing store, a 'drop-in' centre and an old people's club. At the same time, they also collected anything and everything that could be of use to the war effort, knitted for the forces, unravelled and re-knitted garments for old folk and cut down others and remade them for needy children. As if this was not enough, members of the WVS had been trained in how to run emergency rest centres in case Frome was ever bombed, as well as being taught how to cook meals in field kitchens should the need arise. In short, they could turn their hand to anything where help was wanted and in June 1940 that 'help' was required by Major General Montgomery.

Montgomery would later praise the WVS for their mammoth effort during his stay in the town, having on average fed 'fifteen thousand men every twenty-four hours'. At the same time, their transport section, which had ferried evacuees – children and adults – at the start of the conflict to their host families in outlying areas, was also able to be of immediate assistance to the

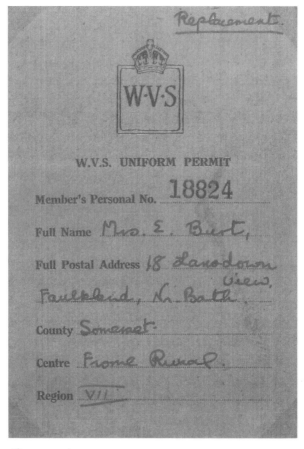

A WVS uniform permit.

new arrivals. Montgomery and his officers of the 3rd Division had arrived with no transport, but with the units scattered in villages in Somerset, Wiltshire and Dorset, he required some way of enabling his staff to keep in touch with them:

> A request was made for some voluntary cars and drivers and, at once, fifteen cars were at their disposal. Later a roster was arranged from a list of over thirty volunteers to work in four-hourly shifts from 9am to 9pm (or at such other hours as were needed), many cars on the morning shift being kept out all day. This was continued for a fortnight, with fewer cars being used as new transport arrived, until the division was completely re-equipped and left the district. Several thousand miles were run – one car alone doing over a thousand miles in the fourteen days.

Meanwhile, the return to France now had a date. Montgomery and his 3rd Division would join up with the remaining British forces on 20 June 1940. However, on 15 June, Montgomery was summoned to London for a meeting in which he was told that the plan had been cancelled and, instead, he and the 3rd Division were to stay in England in order to defend the coast against a now anticipated invasion of Britain by Germany.

Montgomery returned to Frome and gathered all his officers together. On 17 June, at 9.50 am, according to Hamilton:

> Bernard addressed all 466 officers of the 3rd Division – the first of his great wartime addresses to large audiences and prefaced by a new rule: namely that there must be no coughing or throat-clearing once he began to speak. It was the first sign of Bernard's realisation that, to command a large body of men successfully, he must become known by them all, not only by sight as in unit inspections, but by his ideas and their presentation.

By the evening of that same day, the division had begun its preparations for the move to its new location: the south-east

The plaque commemorating Montgomery's stay in Frome during June 1940.

The Portway Hotel as it is today, but now renamed Montgomery Court.

coast between Brighton and Bognor. Two days later, on 19 June, Montgomery and his 3rd Division had completely left Frome.

In mid-June 1940, victorious German troops had marched down the Champs-Élysées in the French capital and a few days later, the country surrendered. With France now under German occupation, it seemed almost inevitable that Britain would be next and with thoughts of invasion uppermost in his mind, Churchill gave his famous 'Finest Hour' speech, in which he solemnly announced to the British people listening that 'The Battle of France is over, I expect that the Battle for Britain is about to begin.'

CHAPTER THREE

The Battle for Britain: June–December 1940

In June 1940, with France now under occupation by the German army, the recently-appointed Prime Minister Winston Churchill and his government turned their complete attention to the defence of their country. Preparations, however, had already begun as soon as it became clear that France would fall, with a likelihood that Britain would be attacked next. Secret War Office information, in fact, suggested that the Germans would launch an invasion sometime between 2 and 9 July 1940.

Unlike in times gone by, it was not only preparations for a possible seaborne invasion that needed to be made; if the nature of land warfare had changed dramatically since the First World War, this had also happened in the air. During Germany's dramatic advance across Western Europe, several unprecedented actions had shown the realities of what airborne warfare could achieve. In Belgium, for example, Fort Eben-Emael had been taken by troops landed by gliders onto its roof, while in Rotterdam, when captured by paratroopers, the Germans had also dropped dummy ones to confuse the defenders. These techniques were also used to capture key objectives elsewhere, such as bridges and crossroads, in order to speed the advance of more conventional land forces, and if it could happen over there, it could be replicated in Britain. This meant that suddenly every field, bridge and railway tunnel in England became a potentially vulnerable point and would need to be defended.

In the middle of May 1940, Secretary of State for War Anthony Eden made an appeal to those men of Great Britain between the ages of 17 and 65, who were British subjects and not already serving elsewhere, to volunteer to join a new organization being created in order to defend their homeland. This new force was to be called the Local Defence Volunteers (LDV). In the words of Eden himself, the name described its duties in three words. It was stressed, however, that at the present time it was a spare-time job, so there was no need for any volunteer to abandon his present occupation. Although during its brief existence the LDV would humorously become known as 'Look, Duck and Vanish' (although these would nevertheless be key aspects for any future guerrilla warfare), the day after Eden's announcement, a quarter of a million men registered at local police stations and by the time the organization's name was changed to the Home Guard two months later, more than a million had joined its ranks nationwide.

Frome Home Guard.

Although from our present-day perspective we cannot help but associate thoughts of the real 'Dad's Army' – as the Home Guard also became known – with the antics portrayed by their fictional counterparts on television, the reality is that these volunteers would have been the first and, in many cases, only line of defence against the invading German troops, whether these came by sea or air. Although many of the comic scenarios in *Dad's Army*, which was broadcast on the BBC between 1968 and 1977 but has been endlessly repeated since, were based on real-life situations the two creators had experienced or witnessed for themselves – both were part of the Home Guard during the war – this was not an unkind or malicious send-up. As was made clear on many occasions in the series – and in interviews given by its creators – the men on television, like their real-life counterparts, were prepared to defend their homes and land 'to the last round, to the last man'.

When formed in May 1940, the Somerset Home Guard, as it would soon become known, comprised ten battalions (an additional three would be added in 1943). These were spread throughout the county and on 21 October 1940 divided into two sectors, North and South, and it was the North Somerset sector that included a battalion based in Frome. The administrative headquarters for the 4th Somerset (Frome) Battalion was at the Drill Hall in Keyford. The red-brick building had opened in February 1914 and had seen service during the First World War, being home to, among others, the Frome District Emergency Corps, otherwise known as 'Tanner's Own' after its commander, Captain Russell Tanner.

Meanwhile, the 4th Somerset (Frome) Battalion's 'Battle' HQ was located in the centre of town at No.2 Market Place. Here, HQ staff were responsible not only for the recruits within the Frome companies – which by October 1940 numbered 500 men – but also those throughout the immediate vicinity such as Trudoxhill, Marston, Tytherington and Nunney, along with others further away including Shepton Mallet, Pilton and Radstock. Each man wore on his uniform, after he received one, shoulder flashes to designate which Home Guard battalion he

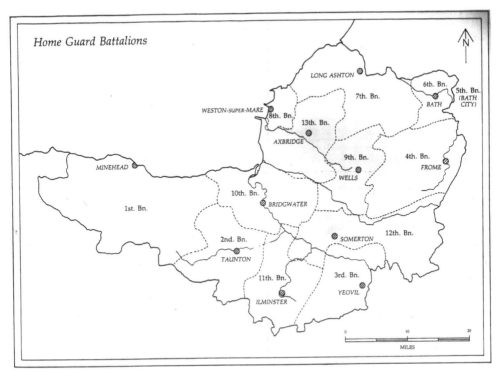

There would eventually be thirteen Somerset Home Guard battalions.

belonged to – in Frome's case No.4 – along with the letters SOM above it, which denoted Somerset.

According to Mac Hawkins in his book *Somerset at War*, the 4th Somerset (Frome) Battalion's commanding officer throughout its existence was Lieutenant Colonel Huntley G. Spencer, TD, DL, his second-in-command being Major T.T. Forster MC. Each battalion was allowed certain paid officers and included what was known as a gas officer. In Frome this was Lieutenant E.S. Robbins, although thankfully his official services were never required.

The men who responded to Eden's appeal back in May ranged from those of school-leaving age to old-time war veterans; their combined force brought with them youthful exuberance and immense military experience. One of these 'youngsters' was 17-year-old Don Perry, who had been evacuated to Frome

The Home Guard marching down Bath Street.

with Coopers' Company's School the previous year and had witnessed the tired and despondent soldiers returning from Dunkirk. 'Soon after that Dad's Army was formed, and we 17-year-olds were allowed to join; a lot of Private Pikes!' He later recalled: 'I also delivered mail at Christmas time, and had an early morning newspaper round in the town; 5 shillings a week was the pay!' This Home Guard volunteer-cum-newspaper-boy and postman was certainly fit, as he would also later recount that he used to cycle back to London from Frome – a journey of around 100 miles – in the school holidays.

At the other end of the age range – and wartime experience – were men like Ernest White DCM. Born in Maiden Bradley in the early 1880s, Ernest William White had joined the Wiltshire Regiment as a young man and had seen action in South Africa during the Boer War and was later stationed in India. In December 1914, after the start of the First World War, Private

First World War veteran Ernest White.

White rejoined the 1st Battalion, Wiltshire Regiment and in March 1915 took part in the attack on Spanbroekmolen, Lindenhoek, in Belgium. This was a support attack to the main offensive taking place at Neuve Chapelle and from their position the rumble of the ongoing battle could be heard. At 8.40 am on 12 March 1915, the 1st Wiltshire and 3rd Worcestershire battalions launched the attack. The casualties suffered by both units were severe, but during the intense fighting Private White engaged in an act of bravery that would later be recognized with the Distinguished Conduct Medal. The DCM was established during the Crimean War by Queen Victoria and given for 'distinguished, gallant and good conduct in the field'; it was the 'other ranks' equivalent to the Distinguished Service Order (DSO) awarded to commissioned officers. As part of a fifty-man bomb-throwing party ordered to attack a German position, Ernest and his comrades were repelled, with many deaths (out of the fifty men, only four survived). On their retreat, however,

Ernest White's medals from the First World War.

Private White located a gun at the top of a hill and held the position, killing many Germans in the process, until relieved by the rest of his regiment. It was for this action that he was awarded the DCM, the citation in the *London Gazette* reading as follows:

> His Majesty the King has been graciously pleased to approve the award of the DCM to No.5814 Pte E.W. White for conspicuous gallantry and coolness during the assault of Spanbroekmolen 12/3/15 in bringing a machine gun into action under very heavy fire under very difficult circumstances after another had been shot in the attempt.

The award must have been bittersweet for Ernest, though, as his wife had died in childbirth a week before the attack. The baby girl lived, however, and was brought up by his in-laws.

The rest of the war saw Private Ernest White gassed, suffer deafness and overcome a bout of bronchitis, as well as spending time with a machine-gun company, before rejoining the Wiltshire Regiment and serving in the post-war period in China. By now, he had been promoted to lance corporal and was presented with a large marble and statue clock by his fellow corporals of the

2nd Battalion, Wiltshire Regiment as a 'token of esteem' on his 'retirement'. After leaving the army in 1920, Ernest came with his wife, having remarried the year before, to live for a time at Nightingale Cottage at Orchardleigh, where he worked on the estate for its owners, the Duckworths. During the remainder of the interwar period, he first lived at Goose Street, Beckington while working for Seymours Court Farm, before moving to 10 Whittox Lane and being employed by Singers. After the Second World War began and the LDV was announced by Anthony Eden, Ernest, along with his son Joseph (from his second marriage) immediately volunteered and joined the 4th Somerset (Frome) Battalion.

Home Guard duties were mainly to protect strategic points and buildings, taking over this responsibility from the 5th Dorsets who were then able to be deployed elsewhere. These duties mainly took place throughout the night and could lead to sometimes farcical and comic situations. 'We used to guard the local water works overnight – went to sleep standing up most of the time!' remembered one member of the Home Guard

Frome Home Guard being inspected in the Market Place.

member, while another recalled being part of a unit dispatched to guard the Post Office in Market Place:

> Our oldest member was an ex-Boer War Veteran who lived alone and was glad of the company and the warmth of our fire. There was at that time some fear of enemy parachutists. We were armed with rifles and instructed to challenge loudly anyone who entered the Square in the small hours with: 'Who goes there? Advance friend and be recognised!' This was taken seriously by one and all, until one night an exasperated shop-owner flung open his bedroom window and shouted: 'When you lot have finished playing at soldiers we might be able to get some sleep!'

Weekly orders for the Frome Home Guard would be printed in the *Somerset Standard* and a typical one, commencing Sunday, 4 August 1940, began with a 10.00 am Church Parade at St John's Church, preceded by a parade with rifles at the Mary Bailey Playing Fields and an inspection by the battalion commander. This was followed on the Monday evening with a drill demonstration at the Cricket Field, Rodden Road, which all sections could attend, while the rest of the week consisted of training and musketry for individual sections from 7.00 pm at the Keyford Drill Hall. On Tuesday the Vallis and Butler & Tanner sections were down to attend, with the Waterworks & Post Office, Chapmanslade and Wessex and the Marston and Reservoir sections scheduled for Wednesday, Thursday and Friday evenings respectively. It was also announced that firing on the range would 'continue for those Squads and Sections which have not yet fired', along with a reminder that 'Armlets may be drawn and retained by all members...[and that] when carrying a rifle an armlet should always been worn.' Preliminary notice was also given of an inspection on the following Sunday by Field Marshal Lord Birdwood. Later in the month, a route march for all sections would be announced, as well as a field exercise for the defence squads in cooperation with the military forces. The location of squad notice boards was also given and included those at 'Ridgegrove', Rodden Road, Toop's Shop, Badcox, Sumner's Shop, Berkley Road, the Great Western Hotel and the Mason's Arms, while members of the Great Western Railway Section could view their notices on a board located on the passenger platform at the railway station. The orders were signed by 'A' (Frome) Company's Commanding Officer, Major R.W.H. Vallis MBE.

Although the Home Guard would eventually become a fully trained fighting force, whose numbers equalled that of the actual army, to start with, weapons, uniforms and other necessary equipment required to fight the Germans would be sadly lacking. Pitchforks and home-made weapons, along with armbands, would be the order of the day. Certain platoons in more rural areas, however, were fortunate in that many of their members already owned firearms, having such occupations as farmer or gamekeeper, these firearms normally being shotguns or rifles. It was soon found these former guns could be made even more lethal by pouring wax into the cartridge to prevent the shot from spreading. The firm of Eley, which made the cartridges for these guns, even took up the idea and began producing cartridges with a single solid ball rather than multiple shot. This shortage of weapons in less rural areas would soon be rectified, however, when a large detachment of machine guns arrived from America (which, reputedly, was captured by the FBI from gangsters). At the same time, Home Guard companies underwent training and were expected to learn such German expressions as '*Hande hoch!*' ('Hands up!'), '*Waffen hinlegen*' ('Throw down your weapons') and '*Ergebt euch*' ('Surrender'). Whether this was, in retrospect, a wise move is open to question, as calling out into the darkness in German might well have led to tragic consequences.

Although there was every confidence that members of the Home Guard would lay down their lives in defence of their country, the possibility of a successful German invasion upon English soil, either by sea or air, had to be taken into consideration. With this in mind, and with the intention of impeding the enemy's movement across the country, the government approved

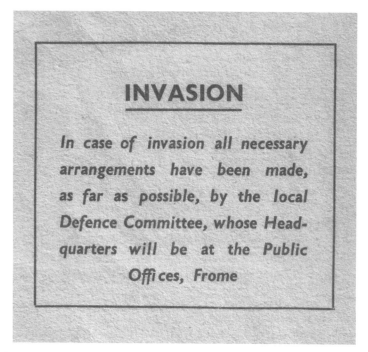

INVASION

In case of invasion all necessary arrangements have been made, as far as possible, by the local Defence Committee, whose Head-quarters will be at the Public Offi ces, Frome

Perhaps over-optimistic reassurance being offered against the possibility of invasion.

what were officially called 'GHQ stop-lines' and the majority of these defences were constructed over the fine summer of 1940 by private contractors. This was a series of fixed defences to run across southern Britain, blending in with their surroundings, in order to impede – or ultimately 'stop' – the enemy's progress.

Each 'stop-line' was named after a colour and a trio of these, or at least varying parts, lay in Somerset. 'White' ran from Bridgwater Bay to Lyme Bay (and was also known as the Taunton Stop-line), while 'Green' was between Gloucester and Bridgwater Bay facing west, before turning east along Wellow Valley to Freshford, facing south. The remaining one in Somerset, or at least a section of it, was 'Yellow'. This began at Freshford and ended up at Salisbury in Wiltshire, having followed the valleys of the Frome and Wylye rivers. The 'Somerset' part of the Yellow Stop-line went across the county border at

Witham Friary, having first gone through the centre of Frome. Included in the Yellow Stop-line defences were several pill-boxes (including ones at Innox Hill, Iron Mill Lane, Spring Gardens and Blatchbridge), concrete blocks at Wallbridge Mill and anti-tank ditches (such as one at West Woodlands). At the same time, the town itself was to be turned into a tank-proof 'island', with all roads leading in and out to be heavily defended by anti-tank guns and rifles.

At some point during the construction of the stop-lines, and no doubt Frome's own defences, a new policy was adopted: that of having a central reserve force that could move to wherever enemy landings were taking place. It was then realized that the various stop-lines, intended to impede and stop the Germans, could easily do the same to our own forces instead and so much of them was either not finished or the sections that had been were dismantled as far as possible. To some degree, it was the same

The Yellow Stop Line shown coming through Frome.

A pill-box at Lullington, part of the Yellow Stop Line which ran through Frome.

Anti-tank obstacles at Wallbridge; part of the Yellow Stop Line but now removed.

with the notion of removing sign-posts to confuse the enemy. Faced with the possibility of German troops being deposited in Britain by various means, the Government ordered local authorities to remove, or deface anything which might help them to find their way around the country. Many signs in the town and the surrounding areas were removed altogether, while others were altered so all the 'fingers' pointed the same way. Whether these measures would have 'confused' the German troops on their arrival, we will never know, but they certainly did confuse the allied forces – both our own and those of the Americans – who found themselves stationed nearby during the war. At the same time, however, these precautions were also part of a larger strategy, meant to deny any German spies or fifth columnists potentially useful information.

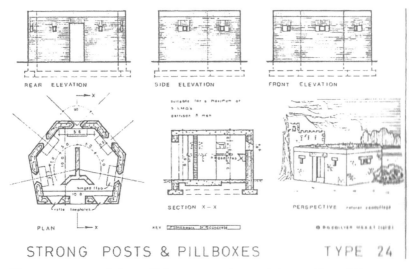

There were many of these pill-boxes erected around the outskirts of Frome.

The term 'fifth columnist' had only recently entered the wartime vocabulary, having been coined during the recent Spanish Civil War. It referred to the members of collaborationist groups native to one country, although really working for another. The phrase had originally been said about the inhabitants of a city to which enemy forces were advancing. 'I have four columns advancing on Madrid,' a general is reported to have stated, 'and a fifth column inside.' In terms of the Second World War, it was known Germany already had a number of these 'fifth columns' operating in several European countries and the fear was they were also now in England.

There is possible evidence of such activity in Frome but despite the genuine danger this 'enemy in our midst' might pose, at other times the perceived threat produced unfounded fears and paranoia bordering on the humorous; one householder, for example, who reported their 'fifth columnist' neighbour, had inadvertently mistaken the dripping of a leaky cistern for the 'tap . . . tap . . . tapping' sound of enemy Morse code messages.

In addition to these preparations, an organization was created which was so secret that only in the last few years has its existence even been officially acknowledged and thus become relatively

more known. Even today, however, the researcher aiming to
delve into its structure, activities and personnel often finds
themselves entering a web of mystery and misinformation, where
details can be at best incomplete or even contradictory, at worst
non-existent. What is now definitely known for certain is during
that summer of 1940, with Hitler and his army poised across the
English Channel, the government instigated a British Resistance
Organisation. On 2 July 1940, all the irregular warfare agencies
in Britain amalgamated into a single agency. The result became
what was known as Auxiliary Units – the name deliberately
vague – whose sole purpose, if a successful invasion happened,
was to do everything possible to harass the enemy within its
newly-gained territory by blocking roads, setting booby-traps
and destroying food stocks, to more major acts of sabotage at
fuel dumps, communication centres, railways and airfields, even
along with assassinations. It is not surprising, perhaps, to learn

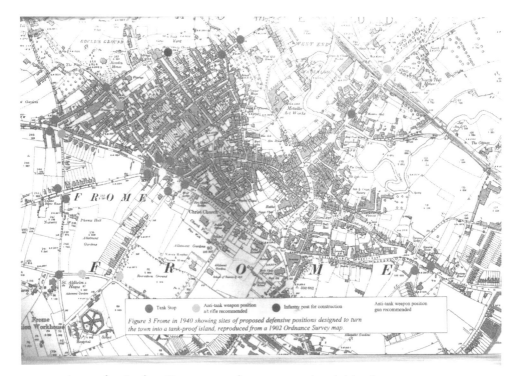

*Figure 3 Frome in 1940 showing sites of proposed defensive positions designed to turn
the town into a tank-proof island, reproduced from a 1902 Ordnance Survey map.*

A map showing how Frome was to become an anti-tank island.

that the life expectancy of any auxiliary called into action was estimated at somewhere between ten and fourteen days.

These 'stay-behind' groups were set up across the length and breadth of Britain and consisted of several thousand auxiliaries, the majority enlisted from reserved occupations. The entire operation was divided into twelve regional sections, with each section led by an Intelligence Officer (IO). Somerset's first IO was Second Lieutenant Ian 'Mad Dog' Fenwick and in time the county became the second biggest network in the country: at its peak, nearly 350 men formed up to possibly 50 patrols operating from 70 secret bases. An unconventional figure, as his nickname might suggest, a demon bowler and an illustrator/cartoonist of some note (his most famous creation being the character 'Trubshaw'), he went to pre-war Berlin after Cambridge as an honorary attaché at the British Embassy, engaged in 'undefined diplomatic activities' (most likely a euphemism for Secret Service work). Some stories later link him with the Canadian Mounties, but what is known is that on the outbreak of war he returned home and joined the Leicestershire Yeomanry. In early 1940 he was transferred to the Royal Artillery and four months later was posted to the elite 60th Rifles of the King's Royal Rifle Corps. Not long after Dunkirk though, on 30 June 1940, he was transferred to a 'specialist appointment'. This, as we now know, was Intelligence Officer for Somerset's newly-formed resistance organization.

The Somerset segment of the British Resistance Organisation was run as two separate sectors – South/West and North/East – each under what was known as a scout

Second Lieutenant Ian 'Mad Dog' Fenwick.

officer. The officers had with them a group of fourteen regular soldiers who gave instruction in aspects of (ungentlemanly) warfare and helped them build Operational Bases (OBs). These OBs were the underground places where the resistance fighters would go in the event of an invasion and from where they would carry out their activities. The Scout Section for the North & East sector, which included Frome, was based in the stable block of Southill House, Cranmore, near Shepton Mallet. Its first scout officer was Lieutenant John McCue from the Wiltshire Regiment, with his team of regular soldiers drawn from the Welsh Guards. McCue would be replaced in 1941 by Lieutenant Keith Salter of the 6th Battalion, Somerset Light Infantry.

The smallest unit of the resistance network was the 'patrol', which usually consisted of anything between four to eight men. These were the ground troops – volunteers to a man – who would literally 'go to ground' in their specially-constructed OBs at the news of an invasion, waiting for their chance to emerge once the enemy was within the territory they occupied and engage in sabotage and other acts. Most had initially been members of the Home Guard and remained so, if only to the point of continuing to wear the uniform, as this would supposedly afford them protection under the Geneva Convention. However, as Hitler had already labelled the Home Guard 'Churchill's Murder Bands' and threatened to deal with them accordingly, what protection, if captured, any association could offer would probably be minimal, if not non-existent. On their uniform shoulder flashes they retained the words 'Home Guard' but underneath, at least from spring 1943, were the numbers 203 (as in 203 GHQ Reserve), denoting Southern England. However, given the secret nature of the organization and possible capture by the enemy, members of the Auxiliary Units were unlikely to know the identities of others outside their immediate area and the patrols contained within it.

The pioneering work of writers such as Donald Brown and Tim Wray has identified two 'patrols' operating within the Frome area: one at Bruton, the other Longleat. Although Home Guard companies and platoons in the villages and towns around Frome

The armband worn later in the war by Frome members of the British Resistance.

were mainly run from the town with the 4th Somerset (Frome) Battalion's HQ being based there, auxiliary patrol activities in the area seem to have been directed from nearby Bruton in the person of Captain Albert Harry Thomas Hunt, more commonly known as 'Dickie'. Dickie Hunt owned Dropping Lane Farm at Bruton and according to Wray in his book *The Somerset Underground: A History of the GHQ Auxiliary Units in Somerset 1940 to 1944*, was a 'compact, sturdily built and charismatic man with more than a hint of the unconventional about him [but] was energetic and an obvious organiser and leader'. Not only was he in charge of the Bruton AU patrol, he was also the area's 'commander', being responsible for all the patrols operating around the Frome area.

A lot of the members of patrols in rural areas were farmers – who better to know the lay of the land – or were no strangers to guns, and this was reflected in the initial members of the Bruton patrol. Members of this AU identified by Wray (and partly by Brown) include Albert 'Bert' Baker, Edward Edmondson, George Hutchings, Thomas Luffman, Archie Roberts, John Steeds, Edward Smith, Tom Symonds and Robert Francis; Baker and Roberts regularly driving over from their homes in Shepton Mallet to train as saboteurs-in-waiting.

The Bruton Patrol had three OBs, which they used for various purposes. The main one was on Creech Hill, north of Bruton, in a small wood which could apparently sleep up to twenty-five men at a push (in the event of invasion the North/East Scout Section was to join up with the Bruton Patrol), while a smaller dugout in a tiny patch of woodland called Ragg's copse was used as an ammunition and bomb store. The third OB – only to be used in case of emergencies – was located in Milton Woods, near Milton Clevedon village.

All patrols undertook military 'exercises' where and when they could, and according to one member of the Bruton AU Patrol, recounted by Wray, they once paid a 'secret' visit to Frome in the form of raiding the Coldstream Guards' billet:

> The Auxiliary Units had a liaison officer whose job it was to find suitable places and units for us to practise attacks. Apparently the Guards were not at all interested in playing war games with the Dad's Army so we decided to remove our 'Home Guard' flashes and went on the raid anyway. Before leaving for Frome we made up little bags of explosives with detonators and fuses already inserted. These things made a louder bang than a thunder flash but did little real damage. I remember drawing crosses with chalk on all the vehicles belonging to Guards to show where they had been sabotaged. During this practice raid Dickie Hunt, myself and another man whose name I cannot recall approached the Officers' Quarters where there was a big lawn in front and a wall all around the building. We crept right up to the wall and Dickie Hunt whispered to me to throw one of my two sticky bombs. Just as I was about to do this we were grabbed by Guards who had drawn their bayonets. We were questioned but had been instructed to give no information other than our battalion number (203), so we were kept prisoner overnight. At seven in the morning we were released and made our way home to Bruton. After I had eaten breakfast I had to drive a timer wagon over

to Frome [for Vineys of Bruton] and saw several Army lorries driving about covered in chalk crosses.

One of the other AU Patrols within Captain Hunt's 'command' was the Longleat Patrol, whose leader was Sergeant William 'Bill' Buckett, head gamekeeper at the Longleat Estate. The majority of the men within this patrol came from the East Woodlands area, south of Frome, and their main OB was located on Carpenter's Knoll, part of the vast Longleat woodlands. Bill Buckett had been promoted to head gamekeeper at the outbreak of the Second World War and so moved into Gunville Lodge, an impressive stone cottage in woodland about a mile north-west of Longleat House itself. As well as his extended family, his new residence also housed the patrol's store of ammunition, explosives and small arms. Also, at times, the men of the patrol did their musketry training there, apparently firing across the road from the main doorway into a horseshoe bank opposite which, at the time, was the site of two large beech trees.

Some of the members of the Longleat Patrol, identified and confirmed by Tim Wray (and again, to a lesser degree, by Brown), include Gordon Derry, Ken Fricker, 'Jack' Heritage and the Crossman brothers, Bert and Fred. Gordon Derry worked as a maintenance engineer for the Wessex Engineering and Metal Craft Company (Welders) of Merchant's Barton in Frome, while Ken Fricker worked in Houston's Mill, also in the town. John 'Jack' Heritage of Poole Farm, East Woodlands was a veteran of the First World War when he served with the Royal Navy Volunteer Reserve, and the Crossman brothers were dairy farmers at nearby New Church and Cole Hill farms who were also known to be keen pigeon-shooters, which no doubt stood them in good stead during musketry training.

Tim Wray also suggests that 'There is some evidence of a Patrol to the north and west of Frome. Several men not part of the Longleat Unit but known to have shared training with Bill Buckett's men are thought likely to be linked to Great Elm.' One reason he gives for believing in the existence of this other patrol is that

> Situated thirty yards up a railway embankment near the old Fussell's Ironworks at Great Elm are the remnants of an OB [which] sat at the top of a steep embankment overlooking Fordbury Bottom and the railway line to Whatley Quarry. Details are sketchy, but at one time it is thought that a steel door covered the hide.

The author then goes on to describe conversations that he had with relatives of the men from the Longleat Patrol during the research for his book, and through this names believed to have been connected with or part of this other AU Patrol were given. They include Michael Ernest 'Mike' Pike and Francis Henry 'Frank' Smart, who were mentioned by the daughter of John 'Jack' Heritage. Pike worked in Hayward and Taylor's butcher's shop at 19 Bath Street, Frome (Hayward and Taylor also had shops at 3 Stony Street and 33 Catherine Hill) and lived at 16 Horton Street, Frome. Meanwhile, Gordon Derry's widow (interviewed by Wray in June 2002) recalled a young man called Reg Milsom, who was part of her late husband's outfit and worked with his mother, Dorothy Milsom, in a grocer's shop at 16 Wittox Lane, off Castle Street in the town.

There is even the possibility of a further AU Patrol located in the town itself: 'Two other Frome men, Ronald J. Bartlett and Alan Grant Smith are also possibly associated with the second, little-known Frome Patrol...[while] other names that have cropped up in conversation about AU activity in this area were farmers Don Lewis and Roland Golay', the latter also being a policeman in the town at the time.

Whether all of the above names will ever be confirmed as members of the Great Elm or even a Frome AU Patrol remains to be seen, but in the course of research for this book, one of them can be definitely identified as being a member of an AU Patrol operating in and around Frome, along with two 'new' names. This is Alan 'Archie' Grant Smith who, along with Ken

The Coopers' Company's School in Frome 1939 - 1945

Edited by George S. Perry

LOVE·AS·BRETHREN

Coopers' Company's School 1939–45.

Howse and A. Craddock-Jones, formed part of the staff with Coopers' Company's School.

In a 2006 publication about the evacuated Coopers' Company's School's time in Frome between 1939 and 1945, edited by George S. Perry, many former staff and 'old boys' included reminiscences of their time in the town. Among them is the following from teacher Ken Howse:

> When the Frome Home Guard was formed, I was part of
> a unit which guarded the Post Office in Market Square

Boys of Coopers' Company's School and their master.

[*sic*] after dark...[but then] Craddock-Jones, Archie Smith and I managed to get ourselves appointed as a hush-hush unit of the Home Guard whose job in the event of invasion was to lie low in a secret hideout in the woods of Longleat Park, from which we were to emerge and fix plastic explosives and detonators on unguarded German vehicles. We spent several enjoyable Sundays digging out our refuge and carefully concealing it with cut-down tree-trunks. One day we knocked off and went nonchalantly for a drink in a nearby village pub where we were soon asked 'Are you the blokes digging that there hole in Longleat?'

Before long, the Army provided them with a supply of explosives and detonators which they first stored in a shed in the garden of the house rented by the Jones and Wright families. The day before the explosives were moved to their hideout, there was a fire at the house which fortunately did not reach the shed. The Army also provided a large supply of emergency rations including many tins of bacon. 'When I was on night watch in a Navy destroyer,' Ken Howse later recalled, 'I used to think longingly of that bacon and that I would make a beeline for it as soon as the war ended.' But as soon as there was no danger of invasion, the Army reclaimed its stores of explosives and food.

However the invasion finally came, whether by sea or by air, German supremacy of the latter would be essential to achieve any decisive outcome. As history now knows, the 'Battle of Britain' refers to the epic struggle which took place in the skies above southern England throughout summer and into autumn of 1940 between the German Luftwaffe bomber crews intent on destroying British airfields and the Royal Air Force pilots attempting to shoot them down before they achieved their objective. Although the Battle of Britain did not really have a

Coopers' Company's School teacher by day, British Resistance fighter by night!

formal beginning or an end, for military purposes – the awarding of campaign medals, for example – the dates set down by the government were between 10 July (most historians agree with this, as around mid-July 1940 the Luftwaffe began attacking merchant shipping and western coastal towns in Britain such as Burnham-on-Sea) and 31 October 1940.

As brave and courageous as the RAF pilots were and worthy of the later accolades bestowed upon them – 'never in the field of human conflict has so much been owed by so many to so few', as Churchill put it – the Battle of Britain was not won solely in the air. Along with the pilots, there were the supreme efforts being put in by everyone on the ground as well, from the maintenance crews and control tower staff to the designers and production workers of the aircraft themselves. Along with these, there were also those who raised money to build badly-needed replacements, because without enough new planes to replace those lost in aerial engagements, the remaining 'few' would simply not have been able to continue the fight.

One method of raising monies to build new aircraft for the Battle of Britain was the 'Spitfire Fund' initiative, which appeared around the country from August 1940. Frome and District's own 'Spitfire fund' began on Wednesday, 28 August 1940, with a meeting called by Frome solicitor Mr A.P. Ames at the George Hotel. A target of £5,000 was announced and by the end of the meeting, promises of nearly £900 had been received. This included a cheque for £250 handed over by Messrs Houstons Ltd (on behalf of its directors, staff and employees), while other amounts pledged included £100 from both Roads Reconstruction (1934) Ltd and Mr Percy Fussell of Rode. There were also a great number of promises of lesser figures, such as £20 from Mr Ames himself and £10 from a Mr James Avery. Mr Avery, a cattle dealer from Nunney, was the person who coined a slogan for the campaign: 'Spitfires from Frome Spell Hitler's Doom'.

During the coming weeks, the *Somerset Standard* kept its readers up to date with the latest figures and news about the fund and in its 13 September edition, the paper outlined a number of the aircraft's parts and the cost of each. For example, they reported, a donation of £2,000 would provide the engine, £350 a tail and £5 a compass, while those gifting £2 10s would have equipped the machine with clocks. Machine guns, meanwhile, which the newspaper implored did 'such deadly work against German raiders' could be provided at £100 each. The fund by this time had exceeded the £2,000 mark, so the engine at least had been paid for. By 4 October, however, the target had almost been reached as the total collected stood at £4,848 17s 1d and on the front page of the 18 October edition, the *Somerset Standard* was able to report that the target of £5,000 had been reached within less than six weeks of the fund being launched and that subscriptions were still being received. In the end, a total of £5,235 was raised and a cheque for that amount was duly drawn and an accompanying letter sent to Lord Beaverbrook.

The money raised by the people of Frome saw them 'purchase' a Mark 1 Spitfire, No. R7200, which had the words 'Frome District' emblazoned in 4in-high yellow letters on its fuselage. Its first flight occurred on 6 March 1941 as part of 45 Maintenance Unit, but two days later, with seventeen other Spitfires, formed 124 Squadron, with which it undertook operations in defence of Scapa Flow and provided cover for coastal patrols and convoys. Its time in this particular squadron, however, was short-lived, as in May of the same year it was transferred to 340 Squadron and then, in October 1941, joined 52 Operational Training Unit. It was during its time in this latest unit that it suffered the first of a number of accidents which seemed to plague it for the rest of the war.

Another ground-based organization whose contribution towards the Battle of Britain cannot be overestimated was the Observer Corps (like the WVS, they would later be able to add 'Royal' to their title). They were described as the 'eyes and ears of the RAF' and in this part of the country, according to author Donald Brown, 'every minute of every war-time day and night, men and women of the Observer Corps watched the skies over Mendip.'

The Observer Corps had been formed in January 1938 and stood to for a week during the Munich Crisis in September

FROME AND DISTRICT SPITFIRE

TO THE EDITOR

Sir,—I am pleased to say that I have received from the Public Relations Branch of the Ministry of Aircraft Production a photograph of the Spitfire aircraft donated by the people of Frome and District.

The Public Relations Officer tells me in his letter dated the 27th Oct. that this Spitfire is :—

" One of the fastest and hardest hitting machines. It carries eight guns, has a Rolls Royce Merlin engine, and attains a speed of approaching 400 miles an hour."

As this is an official photograph I am sure you will wish to publish it in your next issue, and I accordingly send it to you for this purpose.

The name of " Frome District " is inscribed on the aircraft.

The people of Frome and district are proud of their Spitfire, and as it goes on its journeys of destruction it carries with it their fervent hopes that it will utterly destroy those with whom it comes in combat, and will safely return from its adventures.

A. PERCY AMES.

Cork Street, Frome, 31st Oct., 1941.

Details and photograph of the Frome-funded Spitfire.

of that year. They began their 'constant watch' once more on 24 August 1939 and by the start of the war the following month, the county of Somerset could boast twenty-nine observer posts, mainly sandbagged shelters located at 5-mile intervals, including one in Frome. This was initially located in the Mary Bailey Playing Fields, but would later be moved to the nearby Leazes. It was part of 23 Group, which also included Shepton Mallet, Weston-super-Mare, Radstock and Keynsham, and whose headquarters were in Bristol. The Frome post, like all others, normally consisted of two observers: one in charge, the other to act as telephonist and plotter. Both were civilian volunteers who wore a striped armlet with the words 'Observer Corps' in red letters and normally worked in twelve-to thirteen-hour shifts. There was a direct line to HQ and continuous contact was maintained when any aircraft were going overhead. Once an aircraft had been spotted, whether Allied or German, according to the book *Somerset at War* by Mac Hawkins:

> '[They] passed these visual sightings on to Observer HQ in Bristol to be plotted onto a large map-table. Their findings were phoned through to RAF Fighter Command Operations Room. There they were collated with radar trackings and weather reports to present the clearest possible picture of what was happening in the air. In the event of an invasion,' Hawkins continues, 'the Observer Corps role would have been extended to reporting every airborne landing.'

All Observer Posts within Somerset were equally important, but as Frome air space became part of the route German bombers would use to and from the Cherbourg peninsula to West Country targets such as Bristol and Cardiff, its observers needed to be extra vigilant. This vigilance would be fully employed from the start of August 1940, when Hitler changed his strategy of attacking merchant shipping and seaside towns and ordered Hermann Göring, head of the Luftwaffe, to 'overpower the English air force with all the forces at [his] command in the shortest possible time'. This 'overpowering' was to begin on what became known as 'Eagle Day', and was set for early August. Bad weather delayed it, however, but once Luftwaffe crews took to the air, the extensive destruction of British aircraft, air bases and associated factories began in earnest.

'In 1940, after a scattering of bombs through July,' states Donald Brown in *Somerset v Hitler*, 'war came home to Mendip [and Frome] on the afternoon of 14th August.' On that day,

German bombers crossed the English Channel and headed for a number of targets in the West Country. As they were tracked northwards from the coast they passed over Frome and, like their counterparts in the rest of the county, the town's observers communicated their visual information to 23 Group HQ in Bristol.

Directed by the Observer Corps, including those manning the Frome post, Spitfires of Blue Section, 92 Squadron were scrambled from their base in Pembrey, South Wales and headed into Somerset to intercept three Heinkel He 111 raiders, which they did over the Glastonbury area. In a fifteen-minute action, all three German aeroplanes were shot down; the first in a forced landing between Kingsdown and Charterhouse with a stone wall being demolished in the process. The five-man crew survived and were quickly taken prisoner by members of the local Home Guard battalion. The second crashed in flames at Puriton, near Bridgwater, although the crew bailed out before their aircraft hit the ground; again, all were swiftly rounded up after landing by parachute. The final Heinkel came down in Bridgwater Bay, but due to dense cloud the aeroplane was not tracked as it crashed and therefore its exact location was not known. At least one of the crew was killed – his body was found a month later and buried in a Weston-super-Mare graveyard – but what happened to the rest of the crew and their plane remains a mystery today.

The three downed Heinkel He 111s were not the only enemy aircraft in Somerset skies that day, however, and several were able to successfully drop their bombs on targets in the county, such as the half-dozen high-explosive bombs from a lone Junkers Ju 88 that fell on RNAS Yeovilton, which caused damage to a runway and fuel bowser, as well as injuring a nearby labourer. Other aircraft jettisoned their bombs before reaching the targets in a bid to escape their pursuers and that is what happened with those that fell on Cannards Grave and the Frome GWR loop line near Blatchbridge. The latter would be closed to railway traffic for a while after the attack, not because of any damage inflicted but because one of the bombs did not explode and had to be taken away by the bomb disposal squad.

Although the Luftwaffe had twice the number of aircraft of RAF Bomber Command and almost seven times the number of trained pilots, the British had home advantage in the skies and the German losses sustained in Somerset and elsewhere on this day caused its commanders to return to night bombing, at least for the time being, proceeding with a series of prolonged attacks that would have indirect consequences for Frome.

By the end of August 1940 various sites and facilities in and around Bristol had been targeted, including Filton, Avonmouth and Portishead, but come early September, the emphasis of these bombing raids had shifted. In retrospect, it can be seen as a decisive blunder as by this time the RAF was close to defeat; its pilots and aircraft were being lost at a rate that was not sustainable for much longer. The shift of emphasis, however, occurred when Berlin became the target of a British bombing raid. This so infuriated Göring that he decided to switch objectives and bomb England's own capital city, thus beginning what became known as the London Blitz.

One outcome for Frome of the London Blitz was that many of the evacuees who had left the town during the 'Phoney War' made a hasty return from the capital, along with a further consignment of evacuees. 'We all sat in the hall with our identification tickets pinned to our coats, waiting to see who was going to choose us,' Dennis Hill later recalled on his experience of arriving in Frome as part of what became known as the Second Great Trek:

> Now, the problem was that I was given instructions to look after my two cousins and therefore we all wanted to be billeted together. This it seemed was not possible... however, the solution was made by an arrangement that I should be billeted with Mrs E. Wilcox and my cousins would be billeted with Mrs M. Ashman, her sister-in-law and neighbour.

A more dramatic consequence of the London Blitz occurred on the first day of bombing: Saturday, 7 September 1940. As the capital became the target for German aircraft, it was wrongly believed by the government that this was the signal for the anticipated invasion and at 8 o'clock that night the prearranged word 'Cromwell' that signalled imminent invasion was issued, so alerting Home Guard, Auxiliary Units and other civilian defence organizations to the fact that this was their moment. It is perhaps difficult for those who did not experience it to fully appreciate what it must have felt like to believe that your country, your town, even your home, was about to be invaded by an enemy force and all the ramifications that this would entail.

In Frome, as elsewhere throughout southern Britain, as soon as the 'Cromwell' signal was received at Home Guard HQ in Market Place, the 'word' was quickly spread by runners and telephone through the rest of the areas – from Vallis to Keyford, from Badcox to Wallsbridge, from Nunney to Mells, from Great Elm to Rodden – rousing men and women from homes, pubs, cinemas, dance-halls and other locations where they had congregated on the Saturday night. From here, prearranged and no doubt thoroughly rehearsed plans were then put into action by the 4th Somerset (Frome) Battalion and others, so that well before midnight and then throughout the rest of the night, no one on foot, cycling or using any other form of transport could enter or leave the town without being stopped and questioned by sentries, both Home Guard and regular soldiers. The latter stood shoulder-to-shoulder with their volunteer comrades, all ready to fight to the death to repel the anticipated enemy.

At the same time, boxes of grenades and ammunition were taken to secure points in the town, while men of the Auxiliary Units went to ground, as they secretly made their way out to their Operational Bases buried in the surrounding countryside. In certain areas they were accompanied by the distant sound of pealing bells, as in many places throughout the county sheer panic had caused church bells to be rung as a warning, although in reality they should not have started until the enemy had actually been observed within that locality. After a few more hours of this night-time consternation and high alert, those further up the chain of command, once they realized that they

The Bristol Aeroplane Company at Filton became a regular target for German bombers.

had been premature in issuing 'Cromwell' as no invasion was taking place, cancelled the order. Thereafter, a more stringent system came into effect.

During September 1940 Hitler finally abandoned Operation SEALION – the intended invasion of England – and instead focused his troops eastwards on attacking Russia. At the same time though, he gave orders for the stepping-up of bombing raids, night and day, which were to be carried out against important targets on Britain's western side. As part of this new 'strategy', a series of large-scale daylight attacks on West Country aircraft industry locations was planned and these began on 25 September

1940. One of the targets for this particular bombing raid, as it had been previously, was Bristol Aeroplane Company's (BAC's) plant at Filton, North Bristol. Banks of clouds on the day gave excellent cover and – along with the belief that the intended target was Yeovil – allowed enemy aircraft to carry out their attack largely unimpeded. However, by the time this imposing force, which consisted of Heinkel He 111s and Messerschmitt 110 long-range fighter escorts, started on their way back to France, squadrons of Spitfires and Hurricanes, scrambled from bases in Middle Wallop and Warmell in Dorset, were in the air and rapidly flying north. The British pilots intercepted the German planes in the sky above Bath and a dramatic aerial battle ensued that, although ultimately resulting in several downed RAF planes – three Spitfires and two Hurricanes – and one fatality, no doubt proved a spectacle enjoyed by many watching from below.

After initial contact was made over Bath, the combat moved east towards Frome, with one particular Heinkel He 111 being pursued across the Somerset sky by several British aircraft. By the time Church Farm at Woolverton came into sight, the enemy aircraft was seriously damaged, with smoke billowing from its engines and its demise inevitable. One of the Spitfires – piloted by Sergeant K.C. Holland – came in 'for the kill', performing a victory roll in the process, but just before the Heinkel crashed, a rear gunner, still at his post and firing, shot him in the head and killed him instantly. The rear gunner himself, along with another of the five-man crew, then perished as their aircraft hit the ground in a nearby field and exploded. The remaining crew members had bailed out, but for two of them reprieve was short-lived as they were too low for their parachutes to work properly and were also killed on impact. Only the one that belonged to the pilot *Hauptmann* (Flight Lieutenant) Helmut Brandt fully deployed and he came down safely, although badly wounded, in a field near Norton St Philip and was then captured as he lay on the ground. The initial reception he received was mixed: one of those first on the scene made him comfortable and gave him a cigarette, while others in the quickly-gathered crowd were verbally abusive to him. Then, when taken away in the ambulance, he was apparently given a deliberate 'rough ride' by its driver as he drove as fast as possible across the uneven soil. According to one Woolverton eye-witness though, at least one crew member acted 'quite heroically', as the aircraft seemed set to crash within the village itself, possibly inflicting a large number of local fatalities, but 'all of a sudden it veered away' – apparently just missing the church as it levelled out – and crashed into one of the nearby fields higher up.

Meanwhile, the main aircraft formation to which Helmut Brandt's Heinkel belonged was also being harried by further Spitfires and Hurricanes, and a number of the latter – deployed from 601 Squadron – attacked the enemy south-east of Frome, causing one Messerschmitt Bf 110 fighter to make a perfectly-executed belly-landing across the county border in Wiltshire. The aerial combat then left Frome – and Somerset – skies and continued on towards the south coast, over Bournemouth and Poole, where the Germans lost two more planes.

Frome skies were once again filled with enemy aircraft two days later on 27 September 1940 when a record number of aeroplanes – 850 in total – launched four major attacks on southern England; this time, however, most of the aerial action took place off to the west of the county, between Keynsham and Bristol. This would be the last time the Luftwaffe would send such a large force across the English Channel during daylight hours.

Although there would be further Allied losses due to aerial combat over Somerset soil during the remainder of the Battle of Britain and on through the war due to the continued bombing raids, aircraft also crashed for non-combatant reasons: mechanical failure, human error, mid-air collisions or just plain bad luck. For the majority of these pilots and aircrews, they escaped serious injury or death. Although they occurred throughout the county, there were a number of downed aircraft in the Frome vicinity and during the last two months of 1940 a trio of planes – a Magister, a Tiger Moth and a Hurricane – came to ground in Nunney Woods, Beckington and Vallis Farm respectively, although thankfully all three pilots survived their ordeals.

As December 1940 arrived and the Battle of Britain and associated enemy invasion were over, many thoughts no doubt began to turn towards more festive activities. Christmas 1940 in Frome was, however, by all accounts a rather subdued affair. By now, rationing had been in force for nearly a year and so the usual indulgent Yuletide fare was more limited this year. One local newspaper pondered the fact that sandwiches would probably be the mainstay of many households' parties and advocated that they 'be small and slim, and cut in different shapes'. As for what to put in them, the newspaper suggested that instead of keeping to conventional fillings, several of which they ceded were subject to rationing difficulties, a touch of the 'novelty' might be attempted. This approach was also reflected in a suggestion offered for a quartet of sandwich spreads that used available wartime ingredients: cheese or chutney, sardine cream, banana and marmalade or almonds and raisins being the result.

In the end though, as the *Somerset Standard* could report in its first edition of 1941, novelty sandwich fillings and spreads aside, most gatherings managed a semblance of the festive spirit, especially those that involved children. Boys and girls attending their annual Christmas party at Holy Trinity Juniors, for example, enjoyed both games and refreshments within their 'gaily-decorated' schoolrooms and, on leaving, received a 'goody bag' which included sweets and an apple. Evacuated children were not forgotten either, as on certain consecutive afternoons during the Christmas period they, along with accompanying mothers, were 'entertained to tea in the Co-operative Hall' by members of the Frome WVS, with the number attending over the two days totalling several hundred.

There was also cause for celebration with the announcements of engagements and weddings: the former including the one between Doris Vera Daphne of Lewisham Park in London and Stanley William Norris, only son of Mr and Mrs W.H. Norris of Frome, while the latter saw Miss Joan Morris, second daughter of Mr and Mrs Morris of 'Bon Air', Egford Hill, Frome, marry Mr S. Pitcombe of Wootten Bassett near Swindon. The service

Useful information for every household!

took place on Christmas Day at Holy Trinity Church in Frome and the bride, the newspaper reported, was 'attired in a grey costume, navy hat and accessories to match, and wore a spray of pink carnations'. The reception then followed at the bride's parental home.

For wedding receptions nationwide, wartime restrictions seemed intent on eroding tradition and enjoyment. Along with less time-honoured sandwich fillings and spreads now offered up to guests, the customary buffet seemed sadly lacking, given all the other types of rationing introduced during the previous twelve months (although granted, there was later the great wartime standby of Spam, the imported American canned spiced ham that could be used for filling vol-au-vents!).

To top it all, catering for such events really took a turn downward in August. For it was in this month, on the 5th to be exact, that the Sugar (Restriction) Act 1940 came into being, which forbade 'the placing of sugar on the exterior of any cake after baking.' Worse was to come the following month, when the sale or purchase of any cake 'so treated' became illegal, along with manufacturing of candied peel or glacé cherries. As with most problems, enterprising sorts normally come up with some kind of solution, and in this particular case it was the baker's three-tiered 'traditional iced wedding cake' in cardboard that could take its usual place in the centre of the table. Though not recommended to try to cut a slice, it still looked great in wedding photos for years to come.

What the future might hold for the newlyweds, Mr and Mrs Pitcombe, in terms of the war, was anyone's guess, but they began married life in the knowledge that Frome, along with the rest of the country, had stood firm against the enemy invader and at least would begin the New Year still 'free' to continue that fight.

CHAPTER FOUR

The War Comes to Frome: 1941

At the start of the New Year a notification appeared in the *Somerset Standard* which read: 'Frome Fire Brigade. The above Brigade have THREE VACANCIES in the Regular Service, also several in the A.F.S. Applications should reach the Hon. Sec., H.R. King, 46, Butts Hill, Frome, by Jan. 9th, 1941.' In 1938, Frome's Urban and Rural District Councils were legally required, by the introduction of the new Fire Brigades Act of that year, to provide the services of a fire brigade. In addition, around the same time, the Auxiliary Fire Service came into existence; the latter having originally been formed in parallel with the ARP organization. The Frome AFS, as elsewhere, comprised mainly part-time volunteers that could, if required, be called up for full-time and paid service (a similar arrangement existed in the town's wartime Special Constabulary). In August 1941, these two 'separate' organizations would be amalgamated to become the National Fire Service (NFS), which consisted of full-time and part-time personnel that were male and female (the latter being employed mainly within administrative roles). Their uniform – traditional dark-blue double-breasted tunic – was topped off with a peaked cap of the type previously worn by the AFS.

The newspaper 'advert' at the beginning of January 1941 for additional firemen no doubt worked, as by the end of the month, at the Frome Fire Brigade's annual meeting, it was announced the brigade was at full strength. Service during wartime for

PUBLIC ANNOUNCEMENTS

FROME FIRE BRIGADE

The above Brigade have THREE VACANCIES in the Regular Service, also several in the A.F.S.

Applications should reach the Hon. Sec., H. R. KING, 46, Butts Hill, Frome, by Jan. 9th, 1941.

Advertisement for the fire brigade, which appeared in a January 1941 edition of the Somerset Standard.

members of the Frome Fire Brigade – new or old – meant considerable risk, as they would often be called to attend the aftermath of bombing raids, or even while in progress, in places outside Frome, often spending several hours at a time helping to extinguish fires.

A major raid on the port city of Bristol back in November 1940, after the Luftwaffe had switched to night-time bombing, was a particularly intense example. Bristol was chosen as a target to eliminate it as an 'importing port supplying much of the Midlands and South of England' and nearly 150 bombers set out on 24 November 1940 to achieve this. In all, between 6.30 pm and 11.00 pm, the Germans dropped more than 160 tonnes of bombs onto the city – mainly on the harbour area and nearby industrial plants – as well as 12,500 incendiaries; the result being the deaths of 200 people, 900 others injured, and much of the city ablaze, with more than 300 'incidents' logged by the local ARP control centre.

The weather was so cold that water would freeze as soon as it came out of the hose.

By the time the 'All clear' siren was sounded not long after midnight, Frome firemen were already in Bristol, helping to tackle the massive conflagrations raging throughout the city alongside not only local fire-fighters but also those from eighty other brigades that had been requested from Somerset, Hampshire, Gloucestershire, Wiltshire, Dorset, Oxfordshire, Berkshire, Buckinghamshire, Surrey, Kent, South Wales and London. In addition, 20,000ft of hose was also obtained from Cardiff, Newport, Bournemouth and Plymouth to supplement the two hundred or so locally-available pumping appliances which had been, perhaps not surprisingly, completely overwhelmed. To compound matters even further, the main water supply failed through bomb damage, and water had to be retrieved from the River Frome, among other places. The fire crews, including those from Frome, worked through the night and by daybreak almost all the fires had been brought under control, although a number would still be smouldering three days later.

Other problems encountered by the Frome brigade in attending these regional fires included the fact that their hose was of a different type to the equipment held by other brigades and therefore could not be employed, and during the extreme weather at the start of 1941, when attending another of these fires, water froze almost as soon as it left their 'borrowed' hose and reached the buildings. Although Frome Urban District Council could do nothing about the weather, it was proposed and agreed at their January meeting that 'four adaptors and one connecting head be purchased'. At the same time, while reviewing the previous year's activities, Chairman O.L. Seward said that

> [he] must particularly congratulate the town's fire-fighting services. They had been called to another town [Bristol] on three occasions... and the Council was proud of them. One member of the Fire Brigade, Mr Corp,' the chairman continued, 'had been the driver on each occasion, and had given really good service. They had been on duty sometimes for 36 hours at a stretch, and he thought that a letter should be sent to the Brigade expressing the Council's appreciation of what they had done.

Frome Fire Brigade would continue to help Bristol during the first months of the New Year, culminating in the infamous 'Good Friday' raid on 11 April 1941.

The council chairman also expressed at the meeting that the 'town had also been very well served in regard to all the other services, the members of which had given of their help freely and voluntarily through a very trying time'. Not only had the fire service ventured outside the area to help other towns and cities, but also other members of the Civil Defence services, such as first-aid and rescue parties. In his book *Somerset at War*, Mac

Hawkins says of the 'Good Friday' aftermath: 'Both Taunton and Yeovil sent fire pumps to Bristol. In addition, Weston-super-Mare despatched 3 first aid parties, 3 ambulances, and one rescue party; Frome sent 3 first aid parties, 3 ambulances and 2 rescue parties; Bridgwater despatched one rescue party to the city.'

January 1941 also saw the introduction of another 'fire' initiative and at their meeting the Frome Urban District Council discussed 'The new fire-watchers' scheme for protection against incendiary bombs.' (The 'Fire Watchers' Service' would, like the fire services, undergo reform in August 1941, being renamed the 'Fire Guard'.) Incendiary bombs had been increasingly used by enemy aircraft in raids, dropping thousands of them each time, along with high-explosive bombs. Each incendiary canister contained thirty-six tubes filled with powdered magnesium, a silvery-white metal which burned very brightly and had long been used in flash photography, to which a finned tail was attached, the entire device weighing around 1kg. All the tubes would be put into a specially-designed basket and would be dropped at the same time as the normal bombs. The basket would float down on a parachute and part way down spring-loaded gates would open, allowing the incendiaries to fall out and ignite on impact with a solid object such as a roof. Unless they were extinguished quickly, for example by being covered with sand or earth, they could start major conflagrations.

The need to watch for fires caused by incendiary bombs was therefore imperative and so large numbers of fire-spotters/watchers were required. The Boy Scouts' Association initiated a nationwide scheme – which included Frome – by which patrols of Boy Scouts acted as fire-spotters in their own districts. The patrols consisted between six to eight boys, aged from 15 to 16, under a patrol leader, and would be quickly mobilized immediately an alert was sounded. It had also been decided arrangements would be made for patrols to link up, so that wide areas could be covered.

As well as attending bombing raids, the fire service was no doubt called, at times, to deal with the aftermath of downed aircraft, both Allied and enemy. There had been many crashes in Somerset during the previous year – with a number of fatalities – and these types of event continued to occur in 1941. Early February saw another trio of planes crash-land in the Frome area – following on from the three in November and December – but this time they all occurred within forty-eight hours of each other. The first, a Harvard, landed 200 yards north-east of Rode Church, while on the same day a Hurricane came down at Seymour's Court Farm, Beckington (where Private Ernest White of the Frome Home Guard previously worked before the war). In fact, 4 February 1941 was some kind of black-letter day for downed aircraft in Somerset as the county experienced four on that one day (the other two being at Crewkerne and Bath). Two days later, a Hart shared the same fate at Berkeley, near Frome. Miraculously, there were no deaths connected to any of these incidents. Then later in the year, the nearby village of Mells would be the scene of two crashes, about a month apart, with a more tragic outcome. Although the crew of a Magister which came down near the church in August survived, those in a Blenheim that crashed at Mells Park in September were not so lucky. The three-man crew of Blenheim V5377 – J.L. Nyman, C.M. Pratt and J.L. Rodwell – were all sergeants from 13 OTU stationed at Bicester, and all three were killed.

The skies above Frome still saw many enemy aircraft passing over on their way to bomb targets in the west of the county and on 5 July 1941, a Heinkel He 111 was downed at Great Elm after being shot by a night-fighter from 604 Squadron. One of the German crew died, while the others became prisoners of war. Meanwhile, a month earlier, its neighbour, Mells, lost one of its own. Killed through enemy action, RAF Sergeant Ernest John Montague had only been married a few weeks prior to his death. The 28-year-old was buried in the churchyard of the village church, St Mary's.

Another local airman to be killed in the early months of 1941 was 26-year-old Pilot Officer Reginald Albert Lloyd DuVivier of 229 Squadron, Royal Air Force Volunteer Reserve. On 30 March, he died when the Hurricane he was flying collided

IF YOUR HOUSE IS DESTROYED OR BECOMES UNINHABITABLE

Make arrangements *now* with your friends or relations in the town for you to go to them or for them to come to you, if either of you need a temporary home.

Leave with your friends or relatives the necessary change of clothing and see that they leave a change of clothing with you.

If friends or relatives put you up temporarily, they can obtain a billeting allowance. Application should be made to the Billeting Officer, Public Offices, Frome.

REST CENTRES

If you have not made your own arrangements; or your own arrangements will not work for any reason, you will be directed to one of the following Centres :—

Old County School, Bath Road.
St. John's Hall, Vicarage Street.
Sheppard's Barton Schoolroom, High Street.
Zion Schoolroom, Whittox Lane.
St. John's Senior School, Christchurch Street, E
Council School, Milk Street.
New County School, Bath Road.
Oakfield Road Senior School.
Trinity School, Trinity Street.

At the Rest Centres, you will be fed, clothed, provided with sleeping accommodation and your questions answered. The Centres are only to provide a temporary home for a short period while other arrangements are being made.

3

Advice on what to do if your house was destroyed in an air-raid.

in mid-air with a fellow pilot near their base at Speke. He is remembered on the Beckington Memorial.

Easter 1941 bore witness to one of the most devastating and merciless bombing raids of the entire war on Bristol, while places elsewhere in the county, including Bath and Frome, also directly felt its force. On Good Friday, 11 April 1941, the

Luftwaffe once again attacked the Avonmouth Docks and BAC plant at Filton; this became infamously known as the 'Good Friday raid', although there was nothing 'good' about it. This would be Bristol's sixth but thankfully last major bombing and was witnessed, so legend has it, by Churchill himself. Over that Easter weekend the prime minister was due to visit the city and on Friday evening his train passed through neighbouring Bath, but stopped for the night in a siding just west of Carr's Wood Tunnel near Twerton. While there, it is said, Churchill watched from his carriage window the glow of the fires raging throughout Bristol to the west and, in the other direction, could also see Bath ablaze, the latter through a lone German plane, most likely lost or returning home, having dropped a number of 250kg high-explosive bombs on the Dolemeads area located in the south-east of the city, killing eleven people and injuring a further fifty-two. Not long afterwards that night, it would be Frome's turn.

The 56-year-old ARP Warden William Cole had enjoyed a game of crib and a pint at The Ring of Bells in Broadway, Frome, before going on duty that evening with fellow wardens Ernest Barnes and Jack Berry. As they patrolled the allotments of what is now Queen's Road in the early hours of Saturday, 12 April 1941, they heard the sound of aircraft. Far above them, a night-fighter was chasing a German raider across the Somerset sky, probably in the aftermath of the attack on Bristol. There was the sound of several bursts of machine-gun fire before the enemy bomber dropped the remainder of his destructive load: ten high-explosive bombs and hundreds of incendiaries. They came to ground along a route which included Nunney Road, Broadway, Keyford and The Mount. The effect was both devastating and, in two cases, fatal: at the allotments, ARP Warden Ernest Barnes was killed instantly, while William Cole was severely injured. Jack Berry escaped unhurt. Around them, however, numerous houses, most with blown-out windows, were heavily damaged – some so badly they would become temporarily uninhabitable – with many of their occupants lucky to be alive.

As soon as the bombs had fallen, Frome's Civil Defence services sprang into action. One of the most urgent requirements

A guide to post air-raid services.

was to extinguish the incendiary devices now scattered over a wide area along the bomb path, with many having penetrated the roofs of houses. However, a combined effort by fire-watching squads, Home Guard, police, special constables, wardens and residents, with the help of sandbags, stirrup pumps and even buckets of earth, saw the majority of them put out promptly. The fire service attended the one or two more major outbreaks, but again these were contained successfully.

Meanwhile, injured ARP Warden William Cole had been taken to the 'Red Triangle' first-aid post situated in nearby Mary Bailey Playing Fields and from there was transferred to the Frome Victoria Hospital in Park Road. He underwent an operation the following day to remove shrapnel from his spine, but sadly died of his wounds a couple of days later on Tuesday, 15 April. He was buried at Christ Church in Frome and is remembered on the roll of honour in the town's Memorial Hall.

A report in the following edition of the *Somerset Standard* outlined the details of the attack, but did not identify Frome itself, merely heading its account: 'Bombs on South-West Town'. They relayed the fact that the incendiaries had been dealt with 'expediently' and also the appreciation expressed over 'the promptitude with which the Council, local builders and public utility services tackled such problems as first-aid repairs to the considerable number of damaged houses, the ensuring of the continuance of public services, and the many administrative details for the welfare of residents affected by the bombing.'

The newspaper also reported the fact that the next morning 'another high-explosive bomb, obviously dropped the same time as the others, without going off, exploded between two houses in the same vicinity. One house was completely demolished, and two adjoining houses severely damaged.' These properties had already been damaged by the bombs which had fallen earlier and so had already been evacuated.

As bad as owners no doubt felt regarding the damage to their houses and of course the families of Ernest Barnes and William Cole over their tragic loss, this solitary bombing would

SUMMARY OF ADDRESSES YOU SHOULD KNOW:

Clerk of the Council, Mr. H. J. Allard.
Removal of furniture from bomb-damaged property.
Information regarding air raid casualties
Air Raid Damage, Claims.

Surveyor to the Council, Mr. B. H. Parkes, and Salvage Officer.
First Aid Repairs to Houses.
Lost Articles.

Sanitary Inspector.—Mr. A. J. Bell
Food Contamination.

Billeting Officer.—Mr. A. S. Reynolds.

Public Offices, Frome.

Telephone Frome 48

Relieving Officer.—Mr. C. A. Chapman,
Telephone, Frome 25.

Food Office.—Badcox, Frome. Telephone, Frome 551.

National Registration Enquiries.
Employment Exchange.—Capt. Shead, The Bridge, Frome.
Telephone, Frome 101.

Chief Regional Officer.—19, Woodland Road, Bristol, 8.

Fire Station.—Christchurch Street, W., Frome. Telephone, Frome 549.

Police Station.—Christchurch Street, W., Frome. Telephone, Frome 2211.

Assistance Board.—Area Officer, 48, Town Street, Shepton Mallet.

(On the morning after a major incident, an Officer of the Assistance Board will probably be in attendance in Frome to receive applications.)

W.V.S.—Linden Lodge, Robin's Lane, Frome.
Telephone, Frome 133.

Useful addresses in the event of your property receiving bomb damage.

be the worst incident suffered by Frome during the entire war. Also, given the amount of important wartime work going on within the town, the fact that it remained a 'safe haven' and did not become a specific target for the Luftwaffe like Bristol, Yeovil or even Bath, must be seen as a blessing.

BOMBS ON SOUTH-WEST TOWN

HOUSES DAMAGED BY EXPLOSIVES

BUT INCENDIARIES PROMPTLY DEALT WITH.

Considerable damage was caused to a number of private houses in a south-west town, and there were a few casualties—two of them fatal—when a German bomber dropped some high explosive bombs and hundreds of incendiaries, across a part of the town in the early hours during a recent raid. A few houses were so badly damaged as to be temporarily uninhabitable, and in the lower halves of two streets, straddled by a number of high explosive bombs, many houses were damaged. Incendiaries were scattered over this part of the town in hundreds. Many fell in open spaces.

The newspaper report on the bombing of Frome did not name the town.

One of the companies engaged in this 'important wartime work' in Frome was the firm known locally as Evans Engineering. J. Evans & Son (Portsmouth) Ltd had been started during the 1920s by Jack Evans in the naval town of its title, but before the war it had been taken over by his son, W.J. Evans. Portsmouth and its dockyards had been a target for German bombers since July 1940, but the opening months of 1941 saw three major attacks on the city. The first, on 10 January, comprised two separate raids – after the initial one lasting two hours, the several hundred German raiders returned an hour later – and would later be called the 'Night of Terror' by the *Hampshire Telegraph*; 25,000 incendiary and hundreds of high-explosive bombs killed 170 people, injured 400 and caused the destruction of 6 churches and 3 shopping centres. Somewhere between the first and last of the early 1941 major raids on the town, the second and third having occurred on 10 March and 27 April respectively, the management of Evans & Son received a telephone call from the relevant government department to inform them factory space had been allocated away from the bombing. Within twenty-four hours of that call, the first low-loader arrived at the company's works in Goldsmith Avenue and machinery began its journey north, followed shortly afterwards by a convoy of coaches full of employees and their dependants.

The destination for this mass exodus of Evans Engineering personnel and equipment was, of course, Frome; more specifically the Adderwell Works of Butler & Tanner. This printing firm had a long history in Frome, having been established in the late nineteenth century, and the business had been built up to be one of the most respected and successful in the whole of Europe. During their earlier years, their business had been carried out from the Selwood Printing Works in the Trinity Area, west of the Frome centre, but as the firm expanded, the need for larger premises had become paramount. This resulted in their main operations moving across town to the new site at Adderwell, which had many advantages over the one they were leaving, most notably its closer proximity to the railway station. It was to their old printing works in Selwood, however, they now returned in order to allow Evans Engineering to move in at Adderwell.

As it transpired, this relocation would be at quite a cost to the Frome printers. In correspondence from the then chairman of Butler & Tanner to Frome Museum, back in 1993, he wrote that

> I understand we were given three days' notice to clear the site. The bindery was moved entire [*sic*] to the Pitman Press in Bath, and our staff journeyed into Bath daily. Only one of the nine printing machines could be moved, the other eight being boarded up for the duration. The 'lost' machines included all our magazine presses, so this part of the market was lost for good – it seemed not to be worthwhile trying to re-open it after the war as at that time the book market was so strong. The old factory in Selwood Road still contained all our typesetting plant and some printing plant. When the composing room at the Pitman Press was destroyed by bombing, their

staff came to work in Frome. As a book manufacturing operation it must have been totally unbalanced.

Although there are stories of newly-arrived Evans' employees having to sleep on the 'boiler house' floor until they could find lodgings in the town, it was not long before the company and its employees settled in and despite the fact the town already had evacuees and soldiers to accommodate, most if not all employees found suitable accommodation.

The 'important war work' the company undertook while in Frome was indeed very high-level and included production of complete undercarriages for Halifax bombers and Horsa gliders, and undercarriage legs for Hawker Typhoons and Tempests. At the same time, they produced parts for other companies involved in similar operations which included flap controls for BAC at Filton (the target of so many Luftwaffe raids), bomb release levers for the Folland Aircraft Company and machine parts for Armstrong Siddeley. They also made gun mounts for 20mm Hispano-Suiza machine guns, many of which were earmarked for the roofs of factories elsewhere in the country, and precision products such as hydrostatic fuses for the Royal Navy.

It wasn't only during working hours that men of Evans & Co. helped the war effort though, as many of them spent evenings and weekends in uniform, having joined the Frome Home Guard; so many, in fact, they were soon allowed to start their own Home Guard (Evans & Co.) Company, which at its peak totalled 100 men. They were commanded by Major W.E. Arnold and their duties included the patrolling of factory grounds during the hours of darkness, helping to construct air-raid shelters on site and, at other times, giving assistance to fellow local Home Guard companies with their own duties. The company could also boast its own spigot mortar which, according to the exhaustive and authoritative book *The Somerset Home Guard: A Pictorial Roll-Call* by Jeffrey Wilson, 'would be taken on a special trailer pulled by a works van to Champanslade for practice shoots.' Whether any of these Evans' Home Guard became part of Auxiliary

Patrols operating within the area is not known, but it is certainly not beyond the realms of possibility.

Along with the 200 or so employees which moved from Portsmouth to Frome, the firm began to take on local men and women, and it was not long before the total increased to around 800, at least according to the recollection of wages clerk Marjorie Holly (née Bratten), who was employed by Evans & Co. during the war.

With such a large work force engaged in vital and important wartime production, it was no surprise Evans & Co. became a 'high-profile' firm, warranting visits from such luminaries as Queen Mary and Stafford Cripps, at the time Minister for Aircraft Production, as well as welcoming the BBC many times to the Adderwell site; the latter in order to record concerts for both its *Workers' Playtime* and *Works Wonders* programmes, usually advertised in the *Radio Times* as being 'lunch-time concerts presented to their fellow workers by members of the staff of a munitions works somewhere in England'. An audio recording of one of these concerts, along with cine film taken by Mr Evans himself of a *Works Wonders* concert, the VIP visits and footage of his employees engaged in work-related activities resides with the Wessex Film and Sound Archives.

Although probably the most high-profile company in Frome, Evans & Co. was certainly not the only firm engaged in wartime production in the area, nor was it the only one to have moved into the town from outside.

The famous Carley float (an invertible life-raft) had been manufactured in Frome since 1926, when the firm that produced them, J.H. Nott & Sons Ltd, moved from Swansea; one of the reasons was to be closer to Southampton where all life floats were put through stringent tests. The company bought the Silk Mill at Merchants Barton, which had recently been vacated by the well-known firm of Thompson & Le Gros, together with 3 acres of adjacent land. With a large number of orders for Carley floats from the British Admiralty secured – it was decided in 1925 to carry out a refit of the entire fleet – and substantial investment by the company to increase production capability,

The famous Carley floats made by Nott & Beauchamp.

the future looked set for the newly-arrived firm. However, drastic cuts in expenditure by the government and the beginnings of a trade depression soon after meant the cancellation of the entire order book 'at a stroke of the pen', with no compensation forthcoming to the company. Despite this setback, J.H. Nott & Sons tried to carry on through the continued production of its other products, such as acetylene gas generators, electric light fittings and wrought iron work, and repeated injections of cash by the company's members themselves, but the continued recession finally took its toll on the company and it eventually went into voluntary liquidation in 1930. At the same time, the land, buildings and machinery it owned were disposed of, with the Merchants Barton industrial site becoming fragmented following its sale.

Rising like a phoenix from the ashes, however, D.G. Nott (one of the 'Sons' in the original company title) set up a smaller business known as Nott & Beauchamp, and using part of the firm's former site, continued float production through the remainder of the 1930s and on through the wartime years. Despite occasional setbacks such as the major fire back in October 1939, the company saw its Carley float achieve 'immortality' when it became the 'star' of Noel Coward's 1942 film *In Which We Serve*.

Another 'outside' company which became involved in war work was an offshoot of a Cheltenham aircraft manufacturer called Rotol. Frome Tool & Gauge (as it would later become known) was 'settled' in Crown Yard within the town centre by the Ministry of Supply in 1940 (an initial Vicarage Street site having been found to be too small). The work, from 7.00 am until 7.00 pm, included the making of tools (as part of its later name would suggest) for use in other factories.

As well as all these 'outside' firms, we must not forget the contribution made by more 'home-grown' firms, such as Cockey's, Butler & Tanner (as detailed) and others. J.W. Singers, for example, as they had done during the First World War, turned their operations over to munitions production while once again

Present-day image of Crown Yard.

taking on a large number of female workers; and cloth producer Houston's premises were used as a store by Bristol Aeroplane Company (BAC); most likely this included the parts made for them by Evans Engineering.

In June 1941, 'War Weapons Week' took place under somewhat 'controversial' circumstances. At a public meeting held in April, Mr A.P. Ames, a local solicitor and part of the District Savings Committee, the organization which had arranged the meeting, announced to the audience that Frome Urban District Council had 'taken the view that they were the proper persons to run a War Weapons Week' and so the only thing Mr Ames felt was practical was for the District Savings Committee to work with the council to make it a success. At the same meeting it was decided to hold the 'War Weapons Week' from 17 May through to 24 May 1941 and the target should be £200,000 (based on £10 per head of an estimated 20,000 population). This was a huge increase on the £5,000 target of the Spitfire Fund the previous year, but there was confidence it could be achieved.

At the beginning of May 1941, however, it was reported in the *Somerset Standard* that 'War Weapons Week' had been postponed after a decision had been taken at an emergency meeting of the Frome Urban District Council. A statement issued by the FUDC read: 'At an emergency meeting of the Council the following resolution was passed: "That owing to the short time at our disposal to make the necessary arrangements, the proposed War Weapons Week for Frome and District be postponed."' In the following week's edition (9 May), however, this statement was 'challenged' by Mr Ames. 'Last week there was a notice in the Press that the Urban District Council were not going to take the thing up,' Mr Ames was reported as having said. 'They stated it was done in conformity with the advice of the Regional Commissioner. It was most unfortunate at the time the paragraph was being printed the Regional Commissioner was telephoning me from Exeter asking me if I could organise it.'

Within a couple of days of the telephone call between Mr Ames and the Regional Commissioner, the former had organized another meeting, held again at the George Hotel. At this meeting, it was decided to form a 'War Weapons Week' committee under the chairmanship of Mr Ames, and set the target at £100,000. The week would run between 7 and 14 June 1941. It would be an 'absolute disgrace,' Mr Ames had told the audience at the hastily-arranged meeting, 'if Frome was the only town in the country that did not help the Government in the war.'

War Weapons Week duly took place – comprising another huge programme of events, along with the undivided attention of Frome's MP, Mavis Tate – and during those seven days the people of Frome and the outlying areas raised a staggering £253,000, more than two and half times the target and enough to purchase more than fifteen bombers. Indeed, the surrounding villages by themselves had managed to achieve the original figure alone.

It was also in June 1941, a couple weeks after War Weapons Week, a well-known Frome sportsman was reported missing in action by the *Somerset Standard*, while later that year, in the same newspaper, it was announced he must now be presumed dead. In fact, Sergeant Hubert George Sharpe had been killed in action on 12 May on his return from a bombing mission on the town of Bremen. Although from Bath, Hubert Sharpe had moved to Frome and been employed by the town's Western Electricity Company for several years prior to the war. He had been an active participant in sports, becoming a member of the Frome swimming club and a keen water polo player, regularly taking part in the town's annual galas. At the same time, he was also a member of both the Frome and Bath operatic societies. Less than three months before he died, he had married Katherine Coles, who was the only daughter of Mr and Mrs J.H. Coles of Innox Hill, Frome; her father was a well-known local auctioneer and estate agent. After joining the RAF and gaining his wings, at the end of 1940 Hubert Sharpe was assigned to 58 Squadron of Bomber Command, a heavy bombing unit operating out of their base at Linton-on-Ouse. On returning from the night raid on 12 May, the Armstrong Whitworth Whitley bomber he was co-piloting became the target of enemy gunfire and was badly shot up. Some of the crew, including Sergeant Sharpe, managed to bail out, but his body was found a few months later after being washed ashore in the Frisian Islands.

Other men with a Frome connection killed in action in May 1941 included two naval personnel: Ordinary Seaman Jack Irish, remembered on the Frome College Memorial plaque, who died while serving on board HMS *Jersey*; and Stoker 1st Class Henry Stanley Kellaway from Lower Keyford, Frome, who was on the submarine HMS *Usk*. Henry Kellaway's younger brother Leslie had died the previous year while serving aboard the submarine HMS *Orpheus*. It is believed that both Kellaway submarines were lost to mines.

There were also fatalities in the same month as War Weapons Week. Sergeant Ronald Seward Bunce of the Royal Air Force Volunteer Reserve was killed in action on 9 June 1941 while serving in a Wellington bomber of 9 Squadron, based at Hornington, Suffolk. He died during an armed reconnaissance sortie off the Belgian coast at Zeebrugge. Ronald was the son of Arthur and Daisy Bunce of 'Grassmere', The Butts, Frome and the family were retailers of footwear with a shop at 14 Stony Street in the town. They also had strong connections with the Wesley Methodist Church.

Nine days later, 20-year-old Private Maurice Courtney inexplicably died when, according to David L. Adams, he 'accidentally drowned whilst bathing in a river near where he was stationed'. Born in Dorset but coming to Frome with his parents in 1937, he quickly settled in and worked for a time at the St Ivel Dairy and then for Roads Reconstruction Ltd, as well as being a keen member of the local cycling club. Before volunteering for the Royal Army Ordnance Corps in April 1941, he had been a member of the Home Guard since its formation the previous year. He is buried at Holy Trinity Church, Frome and is remembered at the Memorial Hall. At the end of the same month, during the Syrian campaign, Trooper John Lewis Hoddinott of the 1st Calvary Division (Royal Armoured Corps) died of wounds received during the bitter and intense fighting. The 22-year-old soldier was the son of Harold John and Annie Dorothy Hoddinott of Witham Hall, Witham, near Frome.

One of the many guides to wartime cookery that was published.

Throughout the war, the Ministry of Food issued a plethora of publications: mostly leaflets and booklets containing information and advice regarding all aspects of foodstuffs, from its preparation, storage and reduction of waste to more general household tips and recipes. All of this was written in a (supposedly) friendly and

Although the intention was worthwhile, most guides had a patronizing tone.

'homely' rhetorical style intended to combine practicality with patriotism, but most of the time ended up being just downright patronizing. For most working-class housewives, having to cook on a tight budget in pre-war years had taught them more than those in the Ministry of Food were ever likely to know. At the same time, alongside the Ministry of Food's regular 'Food Facts' bulletins, many newspapers and magazines published their own 'cookery books', with the *Daily Mirror*'s *Wartime Cookery*, published in 1939, being one of the first.

As summer turned to autumn and on towards Christmas, no doubt thoughts once again turned to what to serve as family festive fare; although this was perhaps helped to a small degree at the start of December, at least in terms of having some choice, when the Ministry of Food introduced the points rationing system. Every holder of a ration book received sixteen points a month, later raised to twenty, to 'spend' as they wished on items such as canned meat, fish and vegetables; then later rice and other foodstuffs including canned fruit, condensed milk, breakfast cereals and biscuits. If the introduction of this 'points system' gave a 'choice' to women's lives, however slight, then the introduction of another aspect of wartime, later in December, provided women (or at least certain sections of them) with a more major decision to make.

On Thursday, 18 December 1941, the National Service (No.2) Act became law. This essentially meant all single (or childless widowed) women between 20 and 30 years of age (amounting to 1.7 million women) were now eligible to be called up, and through the introduction of this Act, Britain became the first country in the world to conscript women. The 'choice' women liable for military service now had was which one of the women's auxiliary services they should join. It wasn't always clear-cut, but in theory they could choose to join the Auxiliary Territorial Service (ATS), the Women's Royal Naval Service (WRNS), or the Women's Auxiliary Air Force (WAAF). Alternatively, they could go into an aspect of Civil Defence or an industrial job; normally the latter meant working in a munitions factory.

Although this enforced call-up of women was something of a double-edged sword, the quest for female emancipation, which had made giant strides in the First World War and beyond, now gathered further momentum due to this Act in the present conflict. Not that the women of the Frome district or elsewhere needed the mainly male government to pass a National Act in order for them to 'do their bit' for the war. As in the 1914–18 conflict, women were only too glad to volunteer and contribute in whatever capacity was required. Many had already joined the various auxiliary groups before the introduction of the Act, as well as a long list of non-combatant organizations including the ARP, Auxiliary Fire Service, Civil Nursing Reserve, British Red Cross Society, Women's Voluntary Service, Women's Land Army and Blood Transfusion Service to name but a few.

Earlier in the morning, on Sunday, 7 December 1941, the Japanese attacked the US naval base at Pearl Harbor in Hawaii and in doing so, brought the Americans into the Second World War. At the same time, the Japanese began their Malayan campaign which would result, in little more than two months'

The WLA was just one of several organizations that women could join.

time, the fall of Singapore, Britain's major military base in the Far East.

Two days into the Malayan campaign, tragedy struck the British Royal Navy when two of their battle-cruisers, HMS Repulse and Prince of Wales, both part of Force Z, were sunk. On board the former was 41-year-old Albert Walter James Markey of Lower Street, Rode. Albert had been born in Frome and educated at the Council School in Milk Street, and was the son of Albert James and Ellen Markey of 20 Innox Hill, Frome. He had served in the navy for twenty-three years, having joined in the final year of the previous war, aged 18. Also aboard the Repulse and killed was Cecil Roy Frederick Cottle of 38 Alexandra Road, Frome. The 29-year-old cook is one of the grammar school 'old boys' commemorated on the entrance hall plaque located in what is now Frome College. Cecil Cottle, along with Albert Markey, is commemorated on the Plymouth Memorial.

A few days before the National Service (No.2) Act had become law, in the waters off Alexandria in Egypt, Stoker 1st Class Douglas Henry Seviour of Mells was killed when the ship he was aboard, HMS *Galatea*, was torpedoed and sunk by a U-boat. Although there were 144 survivors, Douglas perished along with 469 other crew. This incident was reflective of the war at this moment in general. Things had not been going well for Frome or the country during 1941 but hopefully, with America now fully on board, this might change. First, however, it would become a whole lot worse.

CHAPTER FIVE

The Tide Has Yet To Turn: 1942

The first *Somerset Standard* of the New Year – dated Friday, 2 January 1942 – included a commentary piece headed 'The Passing World'. In it, the author of the article quoted Tennyson (*Idylls of the King*) to herald the coming year: 'And the new sun rose, bringing the new year' and made poignant political points by comparing the poem's romance and chivalry, which recounted the tale of King Arthur and his Knights of the Round Table, with the present-day situation. 'King Arthur, in the poem, has been wounded to the death by the false Sir Mordred, in an internecine war among the Knights of the Round Table, arising from that disunity and falling away from old standards that has its parallel in the modern world of to-day.'

Further on in the piece, the author applauded the adoption of submarines and buying National Savings' Certificates, but deplored the salvaging of Christmas cards to be made into munitions of war. He found there was something:

> 'repellent in the very idea [as] Christmas cards are emblems of love and loyalty and human affection,' he implored. 'They bear witness not only to the links between friends and families, but to the spiritual beliefs that are being attacked at their very foundations. To turn expressions of human kindness and Christian faith into the instruments of death is surely to make a mockery of

the very things they stand for.' He then proposed that instead there 'is still a more fitting use for them – in Children's Homes and Hospitals, where they are made into screens, pasted into albums, and so on.'

He also alluded to the fact Prime Minister Winston Churchill had recently returned from America – now on the side of Britain in the war – after attending the Washington Conference:

> Perhaps it is not without significance that the great Anglo-American Union, which is now mankind's highest hope for future peace, should have been inaugurated by a man who is himself an Anglo-American Union in microcosm. Mr Churchill's mother was an American, and he himself typifies both the American and the English characters in his own personality.

With America's declaration of war on Germany, Hitler realized only too well he would have to end the conflict as quickly as possible and that it would have to be sometime during 1942, otherwise the overwhelming resources Britain's new ally now potentially brought to the table would prove decisive in favour of the Allies.

Another potential breakthrough for Britain had been Hitler's decision to break his non-aggression pact with Stalin and launch Operation BARBAROSSA – the invasion of Russia – the previous year. This meant that much of Germany's resources was now concentrated on what had become the Eastern Front. The possible speed of Hitler's troops, however, as shown in their 'blitzkrieg' through Western Europe back in 1940, meant in all probability it would not be long before Russia was effectively 'knocked out' of the war and Germany would gain access to its vast Siberian oil resources. It was therefore in Britain's best interests to keep Russia in the war, so as well as playing their part in the dangerous North Atlantic convoy runs, Merchant and Royal Navy personnel from Frome and the surrounding areas now also became involved in the transportation of aid to Russia.

One of these Royal Navy warships assigned to Russian convoy duty was HMS *Matabele*. Back in April 1940, she had joined the Home Fleet destroyer screen in the North Sea. Her duties had included the ferrying of soldiers ashore at Namsos while moving up and down the Norwegian fjords, and screening transport vessels out to sea during daylight hours. Unfortunately, while operating in Norway, she ran onto the Fasken Shoal, although she was able to make it safely back to her home port. The damage she sustained, however, meant substantial repairs were required and during this time the opportunity was taken to add a 4in AA gun. The work – undertaken in Falmouth – was completed by mid-August 1940, but the following April she found herself once again in dock, this time at Barrow-in-Furness, for an extensive refit. The work was completed by the end of May, but yet more repairs were required after the ship ran aground leaving Barrow, which meant she did not rejoin the Home Fleet until August 1941, by which time Germany had invaded Russia and *Matabele* was immediately assigned to helping with aid being sent to the latter.

On 8 January 1942, HMS *Matabele* was ordered to join the escort of convey PQ8. Nine days later, off Kola Inlet, she was torpedoed and sank in two minutes. Even in that short time many managed to abandon ship, only to be frozen to death in the icy waters. One of those on board HMS *Matabele* was Ordinary Seaman Kenneth John Weeks. He had been born in Frome and was the son of Herbert and Ada Weeks of 12 New King Street, Bath. Kenneth was educated at the Council School in Frome and at Alderholt in Dorset before gaining employment with a chain of grocers in Salisbury, Wiltshire. He had joined the Royal Navy a couple of years previously, and was only 22 years old when he died. Although buried at sea, he is remembered on the Plymouth Memorial.

However, it wasn't just the Merchant and Royal Navy personnel from Frome who were helping to keep Russia in the war. Back in the town there were numerous initiatives and schemes to which the population was contributing and the *Somerset Standard* was full of news stories of Frome people's generosity. This included a 10-year-old schoolgirl and the 'Aid to Russia' Red Cross Fund being run by the prime minister's wife, Lady Churchill. Cynthia Day of 22 Wine Street had collected beech nuts and crepe paper and made buttonholes, the newspaper reported, which she then sold to raise money for Mrs Churchill's fund. Having duly sent off the grand total of 7s 6d, she received, a little while later, a letter from the prime minister's wife in person:

> Dear Cynthia.
>
> Thank you very much for your gift, which I have just received. I am most grateful to you for the trouble you have taken to help the brave Russian people in their terrible struggle.
>
> Your sincere friend,
>
> CLEMENTINE S. CHURCHILL.

Many others in Frome donated to the fund as well, including a group of carol singers comprising employees of a local works who raised £20, and the Frome branches of St John's Ambulance and the British Red Cross Society, who were able to contribute nearly £150 after they held a flag day especially for the 'Aid to Russia' fund.

Closer to home, the matron and management committee of Frome's Victoria Hospital in Park Road, where the injured ARP Warden William Cole had been taken following the Good Friday bombing the previous April – although he had sadly died a few days later – acknowledged and gave grateful thanks through the pages of the *Somerset Standard* to those who had donated gifts and monies to the hospital. The hospital had been founded at the time of Queen Victoria's Diamond Jubilee in 1897, and through a fund was able to open its doors in September 1901, being formally opened by the Right Honourable Mrs Duckworth of Orchardleigh. With the war, however, came a scarcity of commodities and so appeals for foodstuffs – fruit, eggs, vegetables and the like – along with other items, became

Victoria Hospital with sandbags.

a regular aspect of hospital life. Thankfully, as recalled in a booklet which celebrated the hospital:

> The inhabitants of Frome in their usual generous spirit rallied to the call, often cutting down on their own rations so that they could donate a small portion to the hospital. Every two weeks the hospital management committee, with their grateful thanks, would print a list of who donated what, in the local newspaper.

One such printed list from April 1942 included the following donations: Mrs Garrett, eggs; Mrs Armstrong, onions; Mrs Cocky, bedside table, greens; Mrs Wiltshire, bandages; Mrs Elliot, rhubarb and onions; Mr Fellows, leeks and cabbage.

Yet not everyone entered into the festive spirit or was doing their bit for the war effort. In early January it was reported a Corsley man, Edward Dredge, had been fined for selling milk adulterated with water. After samples were taken from six of his milk churns, five were found containing various percentages of added water, while later samples taken from the cows themselves proved the milk itself to be above standard. The total amount of water in the milk under scrutiny amounted to a staggering two and a half gallons. Dredge was fined £5.

Meanwhile farm labourer Ronald Moger of Lower Street, Rode was sentenced to one month's imprisonment with hard labour for stealing nearly two dozen fowls from his employer, Mr Harold Feltham of Manor Farm, Tellisford, while a 49-year-old engineer, John Malcolm Petrie, was given a twenty-two-month prison sentence for stealing money from his Frome employers, Messrs Garton & Thorne.

Then later in the month, a 17-year-old youth of Victoria Road, Frome was charged with stealing sixteen grenades and detonators from a store, where they were kept for the use of the Home Guard. On Saturday, 17 January 1942, a night watchman heard an explosion, although on checking he found nothing wrong. It later transpired, after he was arrested following an investigation, the youth had thrown the bombs into Cockey's to 'know how to use them and see what would happen'. He was given one month's prison sentence with hard labour.

There were also many minor offences reported, mainly cyclists fined for not displaying obligatory lights during the blackout – such as Geoffrey Arnold and Muriel Rayney, both of Catherine Street; Arthur Bailey of Keyford; and Margaret Parfitt of Oakfield Road – while motorist Edward Edmondson of High Street, Bruton was fined £1 and had his licence endorsed for exceeding the speed limit.

The loss of the military base at Singapore in February 1942 was a major blow to the Allied cause. Numerous men from Frome and the surrounding areas had been involved throughout the Malayan Campaign – which included Albert Markey and Cecil Cottle who had lost their lives aboard HMS *Repulse* in December – and now many more would feel the after-effects since the victorious Japanese had taken over. On the day of the surrender itself, 15 February, Private Frederick William Fricker died. He was 30 years of age and although the Commonwealth War Graves Commission was not informed of his next of kin, it is believed he was the son of Mr W.J. Fricker of Avenue Road, Frome. He served with the 18th Division, Ordnance Workshops, Royal Army Ordnance Corps, which had arrived on Singapore Island sometime between mid-January and early February to reinforce the 8th Australian and 11th Indian divisions and was captured shortly afterwards with the fall of the base. After the war, Kranji War Cemetery was opened in the north of Singapore Island containing the remains of 3,702 men, Private Fricker among them.

Within Kranji War Cemetery is the Singapore Memorial, in remembrance of those who died during the Malaya campaign and elsewhere, and who have no known grave. It was unveiled on 2 March 1957 by the then governor of Singapore, Sir Robert Black, and has 24,317 names inscribed upon it. One of these is Sergeant Joseph J. Keevil, who died on 1 March 1942 at the age of 32. He was serving with the 12th Battery, 6th Heavy Anti-Aircraft Regiment of the Royal Artillery on Java when Singapore fell. He is also remembered on the Beckington Memorial, where he had lived with his now widow, Hilda.

The day after the fall of Singapore another seaman with a Frome connection and enshrined on the Plymouth Naval Memorial died. Stoker 2nd Class Charles Frederick James had joined the Royal Navy thirteen months earlier and survived the sinking of HMS *Prince of Wales* back in December. He cabled his wife – Mrs James of 4 Paul Street, Frome – in the New Year to say he was safe and well in Malaya, but was reported missing in action after joining HMS *Sultan*. As well as his widow, he left a 5-year-old daughter.

It wasn't just navy personnel from Frome who were dying at sea though, as eight days after Stoker James had perished, Cyril Norman Bower of the RAF lost his life somewhere off the North African coast. Sergeant Bower of 104 Squadron, Royal Air Force Voluntary Reserve was the son of Charles and Esther Bower of Frome and was married to Marjorie, who also lived in the town. Prior to being called up in October 1940, Cyril Bower had been employed by the Midland Bank; first at its Frome branch, then being transferred to Taunton. After undergoing post-call-up training, he joined 104 Squadron, which was equipped with Wellington bombers. During the first five months of 1942 the squadron was stationed at RAF Kabrit in Egypt, serving in the North African campaign, and it was during this time, on 24 February, that Sergeant Bower was shot down. Although he has no known grave, the airman is remembered on the Alamein Memorial and on the Memorial Hall roll of honour in Frome.

The middle of February in Frome saw the start of what had become an annual event, the national 'Military Week' designed to raise funds for the war effort. In 1942, this was designated 'Warship Week', the objective being for towns and cities around the country to loan the government, through initiatives such as National War Bonds, Saving Certificates and Post Office Savings Accounts, the amount of £175,000 which, if achieved, would result in them being able to 'adopt', as the name suggests, a Royal Navy warship. This took place between 14 and 21 February 1942 and to ensure success, another week-long series of events was organized including a Grand Military Procession, a demonstration by the Frome Home Guard of modern war weapons and the 'Thunderbolt' Dance, to be held on the Friday at the George Hotel in Market Place; the latter being named after HMS *Thunderbolt*, the naval submarine the town would 'adopt' if its target was reached. At the same time, for those mothers who gave birth in that week, Frome's Urban and Rural District Councils promised to once again give a Savings Certificate to every resultant baby. As the week unfolded and the people of Frome did all they could to reach their target, most, if any, were unaware of the tragic history which lay behind the 'warship' they wanted to adopt.

HMS *Thunderbolt* had originally been called HMS *Thetis*, but she had sunk during her first diving trial not long before the war. The submarine had been built at Cammell Laird's in Birkenhead, but misfortune had struck even before she reached the water as her diving trials were delayed through technical difficulties with jamming forward hydroplanes. *Thetis* was eventually ready for her initial test and set out from Birkenhead

HMS Thetis/Thunderbolt.

mid-morning of 1 June 1939, heading to Liverpool Bay with Lieutenant Commander G.H. Bolus RN in command. Along with her commander and crew, there were also several other personnel aboard including naval officers, Cammell Laird employees and a couple of catering staff; the latter for the post-trial reception. In total, there were 103 people on board, twice the normal number.

The full account of the incident appears in David L. Adams' book *Frome's Fallen Heroes of World War Two*, but the basic facts are that through a combination of human error, negligence and sheer bad luck, HMS *Thetis* found herself stranded at the bottom of Liverpool Bay. Normally the crew would have air for thirty-six hours, but with double the number of people on board, this was cut to eighteen, most of which was used up waiting for a rescue operation to start. In the end, just four men were brought out alive, the remaining ninety-nine perishing when the submarine flooded and an increase in carbon dioxide instantly and mercifully killed them (rather than a prolonged and doomed struggle against drowning which would soon have occurred); a 100th life would be claimed during the subsequent salvage operation to raise HMS *Thetis*, which was also beset with difficulties and even after she was finally brought to the surface, at the beginning of September 1939, her hulk became beached on a sandbank where it remained for more than a week, while bad weather further hampered and delayed the operation to retrieve all the bodies from her interior.

HMS *Thetis* was eventually brought back to the place of her 'birth', where she was completely stripped and refitted, all traces of her former identity being erased. It was then she was renamed HMS *Thunderbolt* and entered service in December 1940. Although the people of Frome no doubt listened on their wirelesses in 1939 to the rescue attempt to save those trapped inside *Thetis*, they would not have known this was the former identity of the submarine they had now adopted, and adopt it they did, as the target of £175,000 was reached and surpassed; the final total raised being £176,781.

When the announcement of Warship Week had initially appeared within the *Somerset Standard*, an editorial fleetingly queried what connection the town actually had with the navy – humorously stating there had 'never been a Naval review in Pilly Vale River' – before answering its own question through reflection on the fact that thousands of 'Frome boys' had joined the British navy from Nelson's days onward. At the same time, the newspaper continued, captains of the ships of that navy had lived here, admirals of the fleet had been born in this town or its surrounding neighbourhoods, and yet more high-ranking naval officers had distinguished themselves in their naval career and then retired to a well-earned rest in Frome. The newspaper then gave several examples of these naval men: 'Many Frome people will, no doubt, remember Admiral Arbuthnot, who lived at Ightham, now called Selwood Lodge, for some years, and died there September 30, 1913. His presence and voice were absolutely typical of the quarter-deck.'

The newspaper also mentioned the Boyle family of Marston House, Earls of Cork and Orrey, who it was said gave many members to both army and navy, stating that even at that present time there was an Earl of Cork who was an admiral. The newspaper then went on to say there had been several ships named *Thunderbolt* through the centuries (referring, of course, to the ship the town was aiming to 'adopt') and one such named ship, in the mid-nineteenth century, had been captained by Alexander Boyle, no doubt, the newspaper supposed, himself a member of the great Boyle family. The Edgells of Standerwick Court, it was stated, had also provided two admirals for the navy.

Another warship 'adopted' during Warship Week was the destroyer HMS *Vortigern*, the money being raised by Wells. The city's adoption, however, was short-lived, as a month later on 15 March 1942 the vessel was sunk while on convoy duties in the English Channel. On board was Leading Seaman Ronald Frederick Palmer, whose parents had formerly lived at Great Elm. The 22-year-old was reported missing and presumed dead and is remembered on memorials at Great Elm and Portsmouth. HMS *Vortigern* sank with the loss of 110 lives – there were only 14 survivors – and the wreck site is now covered by the 1986 Protection of Military Remains Act.

March 1942 saw another fatality, but this time it was nearer to home and due to an accident. Under the headline 'Soldier Killed When Bren Gun Carrier Overturns'. The *Somerset Standard* detailed the recent inquest into the death of George

The gravestone of George Armstrong.

Armstrong, a Coldstream Guardsman stationed at the time in Frome:

> The circumstances of the death of a 26-year-old soldier, George Armstrong, whose home was at Kingston-on-Thames, who was killed when a Bren gun carrier, in which he was riding, mounted a bank and overturned, pinning him underneath were the subject of an enquiry by Mr. G.H.W. Cruttwell (Deputy Coroner

for S.E. Somerset) at Frome on Wednesday. Evidence was given by the other three occupants of the carrier, two of them describing how they extricated themselves after being trapped in the front compartment. Medical evidence was given that deceased sustained multiple injuries to the chest. Recording a verdict of accidental death, in accordance with the medical evidence, the Coroner said no blame could be attached to anybody. The behaviour of the other members of the crew after the accident had been excellent.

As tragic as it was, even a cursory search in newspapers of the time reveals this type of accident – and resultant military or civilian fatalities – to be only too common. Indeed, there had already been a number of similar accidents previously in the war, including one earlier in this particular year.

The following month, April 1942, Sergeant Francis Geoffrey Huntley, only son of the late Mr Francis Goodfellow Huntley and

Christchurch, which is the location for several war graves from both world wars.

Ada Sarah Amelia Huntley of 55 Somerset Road, Frome, was killed. Francis was educated at Wesley Boys' School and Frome County Secondary School (now Frome College), before being employed at the Rural District Council Offices as an assistant rate collector. Francis joined the RAF as a volunteer in August 1940 and was assigned to 142 Squadron based at Waltham, near Grimsby and equipped with Wellington bombers. He was killed during air operations over Europe and is buried at Rheinberg War Cemetery, Germany. He is commemorated on the plaque at Frome College, unveiled on 26 July 1946, dedicated to the fourteen 'old boys' who died in the war.

The day after Sergeant Huntley's death, another aerial fatality occurred: that of the Tiger Moth pilot who crashed near Frome, at Pound Copse, Gaer Hill. Pilot Officer J.C. Jones was based at Abingdon, along with a Pilot Officer Johnson, who was injured. Meanwhile, the pilot of an Anson who came down on the same day at Upton Noble, south-west of Frome, survived his forced landing. Incredibly, these were just two of the seven aircraft, including Spitfires and Hurricanes, which had their flights cut short throughout Somerset during that particular twenty-four hours.

Back in February 1942, in the aftermath of Hitler's decision to transfer the majority of the Luftwaffe's aircraft to the East, RAF Bomber Command was informed by the Air Ministry that 'It has been decided that the primary objective of your operations should now be focused on the morale of the enemy civil population, and in particular of the industrial workers.' This change of emphasis was put into action towards the end of March, when the Baltic port of Lübeck and then not long after, Rostock, were heavily bombed. Instead of concentrating on harbour and industrial areas, the medieval and historic centres of the cities were also targeted, the majority of which were destroyed. So incensed was Hitler about this wanton destruction that in the middle of April the German leader signed Order Number 55672/42, which instructed the Luftwaffe's High Command that 'When targets are being selected, preference is to be given to those where attacks are likely to have the greatest possible effect on civilian life. Besides raids on ports and industry, terror attacks of a retaliatory nature are to be carried out against towns other than London.' The first results of this directive came on the night of 23 April 1942 when Exeter became the target for German bombers. The following night it was attacked for a second time, but on the next, the Luftwaffe dropped their bombs on a different city; this time one much nearer to Frome.

The City of Bath from the outset of the war had been deemed, like Frome, a 'safe haven'. It had been chosen as a reception area for Operation PIED PIPER and, like its near neighbour, had welcomed several thousand evacuees into its midst. Unlike Frome, however, it wasn't just children, teachers and pregnant mothers who made the city their new home, as Admiralty departments had also been 'evacuated' there during September 1939. At the same time, quarries and mines in the surrounding areas were converted into great underground stores and factories, while several long-established firms in Bath – such as Stothert & Pitt – were engaged in important war work. Despite these potential 'targets', the city was still deemed 'safe' and so

The Bath Chronicle *reports the devastating news.*

did not warrant anti-aircraft guns or other types of defences. This meant that when German bombers arrived on the night of Saturday, 25 April 1942 (and the following one), this latter-day heritage site was completely defenceless. The Luftwaffe carried out three raids over those two nights (as in the Portsmouth raid of January 1941, they returned for a second time after refuelling and reloading on the Saturday night), leaving 417 people dead, several hundred wounded and huge areas of the city ablaze.

Among the 'Bath Blitz' dead was Kenneth Edwin Snook from Frome, killed at Catherine Place within the city during the second night of bombing. The 25-year-old police constable was a member of the Somerset Constabulary. He was the son of Kate E. Snook of 50 Rodden Road, Frome and the late Edwin Spencer Snook. PC Snook had been born in the penultimate year of the First World War and spent part of his education at the renowned Sexey's School in Bruton. After leaving school, he went to work at his father's furniture shop at 2 Catherine Street, Frome, but joined the Somerset Constabulary in 1939. He is commemorated on a plaque at Bath City Police Headquarters and is on the roll of honour at the Memorial Hall in Frome.

In the aftermath of the Bath Blitz, many people from in and around Frome travelled the 11 or so miles north to help their

The memorial in Bath, which contains the name of Kenneth Edwin Snook.

neighbours, along with numerous meals cooked in the town and taken across for distribution to the various rest centres rapidly set up within the bombed-out city. Among the helpers who travelled to Bath during the early hours of Monday, 27 April 1942 was the Frome No.1 Rescue Squad. Beginning at 5 o'clock in the morning, once in the city, the ten-man squad began the 'arduous and perilous' task of rescuing victims trapped beneath tons of masonry and after many, many hours of dangerous toil, successfully rescued people from beneath the ruins of No.1 Catherine Mansions. Although some were badly injured, they were nevertheless alive and were taken to hospital. Having initially arrived at the house, the men of the rescue squad found the five-storey building, along with its neighbour, collapsed and so had to cut their way down to the basement and then on through a partition. After successfully negotiating this second obstacle, the Frome men found a number of people trapped under a tremendous amount of debris, so it took several more hours to successfully bring everybody out of the building.

More than 400 people were killed during the raids on Bath.

The majority of people that went to the aid of Bath had only good intentions and motives, but for some temptation proved too great and several people, including from Frome, were brought before the courts on charges of looting: the stealing of belongings from bombed-out properties whose occupants had either been killed or were staying elsewhere until they could return. One of the Frome 'looters' was a man caught red-handed with a bottle of champagne that he had taken from a house!

The month of May brought with it the death of another Frome man. This was Harold George Ashford, son of George and Esther Ashford. Harold was serving on board the submarine HMS *Urge* as leading telegraphist when killed on 6 May 1942. However, the circumstances surrounding his death, along with the rest of the crew, remain unknown. Near the end of April *Urge* left Malta on passage to Alexandria, where she was due to arrive on 6 May. The submarine failed to arrive. It is possible she struck a mine outside Malta or was sunk by the Italian torpedo boat *Pegaso*.

The official war memorial in Bath.

The following month – June 1942 – saw another Royal Navy ship sunk with a local man on board. Frederick John Oliver was a petty officer stoker on HMS *Hermione*, a *Dido*-class light cruiser that was sunk while on escort duty by the German submarine *U-205* during a joint operation. Operation HARPOON was one of two simultaneous Allied convoys sent to supply Malta in the Axis-dominated Mediterranean in mid-June 1942. Operation VIGOROUS left Alexandria, while the other, HARPOON, travelled in the opposite direction from Gibraltar. Both convoys met with fierce Axis opposition and only two of six HARPOON merchant ships completed the journey, at the cost of several Allied warships, *Hermione* being one of them. The 29-year-old Frederick Oliver has no known grave but is remembered on the Plymouth Naval Memorial.

At the end of June a Hurricane crashed 1 mile south-west of Bruton church. The pilot survived, as did the crews of the Taylorcraft monoplane which came down a fortnight later at Critchell Farm and a Magister, also near Frome, in August. Not so fortunate was Sergeant Walter John Mills of 76 Squadron RAFVR, who was killed in action on 25 June 1942. Son of Frederick and Lucy Jane Mills, formerly of West Woodlands and Frome, Walter had been educated at Nunney and employed by the World Stores in Frome prior to joining up. At the time of his death, Sergeant Mills was a wireless operator/air gunner flying in a Handley Page Halifax heavy bomber as part of the third and final raid of the 1,000-bomber offensive known as Operation MILLENNIUM. The target for that night was the German port of Bremen, with specific targets including the Focke-Wulf factory and the AG Weser and Vulcan shipyards. The Halifax bomber Sergeant Mills was aboard took off from its base in County Durham at 2236 hours and was not heard from again. Although the exact details surrounding the Halifax's fate are not known, it seems likely it was severely damaged through contact with enemy fighters and came down in the North Sea.

Three days after Sergeant Walter Mills' death, the war claimed the life of another Frome man. William John Carpenter is one of the fourteen 'old boys' remembered on the Frome College commemorative plaque. Born in 1917 at Keyford, Frome, William was educated at Christ Church and Frome Secondary schools. He was an active member of the Christ Church choir and the local scout movement and on leaving school became (somewhat fated, perhaps, given his name) a carpenter. He initially worked for E.C. Barnes builders of Long Ground in the town, before his carpentry skills were then employed by the government in Birmingham and other places. Called up, he became a tank driver in the Eighth Army and saw action in the North African campaign. On 20 June 1942, Tobruk fell and the British Eighth Army went into full retreat to a defensive system, the Alamein Line, hotly pursued by the Afrika Korps. In the intense fighting which took place during the last days of June, Trooper William John Carpenter of the 2nd Royal Gloucestershire Hussars was killed in action. He is buried in El Alamein War Cemetery in Egypt. He was 26 years old, which it is said was the average age of all those killed throughout the Second World War.

There were no further fatalities of Frome servicemen throughout the rest of summer 1942, but in October the life of Ordinary Seaman Alec Brewer, among others, was taken in the most tragic of circumstances. Brewer was serving on HMS *Curacoa* when she was cut in two by the *Queen Mary*, an 80,000-ton liner being used as a troopship to transport 10,000 American soldiers across the Atlantic to Britain. The *Curacoa* was an anti-aircraft cruiser escorting the *Queen Mary*. Some 40 miles north of Ireland's Tory Island, the *Curacoa* was ahead of the larger vessel, but because of her lower speed the cruiser was slowly being overtaken and eventually ended up astern of the liner. At exactly 2.09 pm, the *Queen Mary*'s First Senior Officer James Robinson returned from lunch to the liner's bridge and on taking over noticed the *Curacoa* was much closer to the ship than when he had gone to lunch. The *Queen Mary*'s captain told him not to worry, however, as he was certain the cruiser would keep out of her way; the navy was used to escorting ships, he said, and so wouldn't interfere with the liner. Aboard the *Curacoa* though, only now was it realized how quickly the liner was bearing down on them and a collision was inevitable. At exactly 2.12 pm the *Queen Mary* ploughed into the *Curacoa*, cutting the smaller ship in two. Not surprisingly, she quickly sank, taking with her more than 300 of her crew, including Ordinary Seaman Brewer.

Alec Alfa Brewer had been born on 14 September 1923, and was the son of George and Florence Ada Brewer of 76 Selwood Road, Frome. He was educated at the Council School in Milk Street and like Trooper William Carpenter became a choirboy and joined the scouts. He also served in the Frome Auxiliary Fire Service and 4th Somerset (Frome) Battalion Home Guard and was employed by two of the town's butchers: first Hayward's Butchers of Stony Street and then later J.O. Lewis and Sons, Bacon Curer of Whittox Lane. He joined the Royal Navy in May 1942 and at the time of his death he was 19 years old and was a radar rating in the Radio Direction Finding (Radar) position, high up in HMS *Curacoa*'s superstructure. He is buried at Kilmory Old Churchyard, Invernesshire, although

HMS Curacoa, *which was accidently sunk by the* Queen Mary.

he is also remembered at Memorial Hall, Trinity Church and commemorated on a bronze memorial plaque in Frome Wesley Methodist Church.

There was a postscript to this tragedy and it is that although several hundred of HMS *Curacoa*'s crew died, there were survivors, but these looked on in disbelief as the *Queen Mary* carried on, albeit at a reduced speed, as if nothing had happened; the captain, in fact, had been given orders 'not to stop for anything'. A pair of Royal Navy destroyers eventually returned to pick up the survivors some two hours later. Also, the British Admiralty feared the incident would have a demoralizing effect on naval personnel and the public, so the incident was not made known until much later. A court of inquiry, however, would lay blame primarily with the *Curacoa*, but also faulted the lookout aboard the *Queen Mary*.

November 1942 saw the deaths of two men from surrounding villages near Frome during the continuing North African campaign. On the 12th, Leading Stoker Albert Thick from Hemington died aboard HMS *Hecla* – a 10,850-ton submarine depot ship – when she was torpedoed and sunk during the Allied landings at Algeria. Two days later, Corporal Donald Godfrey Heath of Rode, serving in the 8th King's Royal Irish Hussars, was killed in action during the advance into Cyrenaica, Libya. Both men are remembered on memorials in their respective villages. Despite these deaths, the North African campaign had by now turned in favour of the Allies, most notably the victory at the Battle of El Alamein by the Eighth Army, led by General Montgomery (later promoted to field marshal). Back in Britain, on Sunday, 15 November 1942, church bells throughout the land, including those in Frome, were officially rung for the first time since the start of the war, the government having given permission for them to be sounded in celebration of the momentous Allied victories in North Africa achieved by the town's former, albeit temporary, resident.

Elsewhere in the war, things were still not going well. After the fall of Singapore in February, large numbers of people – individuals and groups – had tried to escape to safety, but many were captured. Unfortunately, in the eyes of the Japanese, as one author has written: 'Allied troops taken prisoner were considered unworthy of honourable treatment [and so therefore were] subjected to appalling cruelty and inhumanity at the hands of their captors.'

This 'cruel and inhuman' treatment predictably led to many deaths within the ranks of Allied prisoners of war and two of these, with Frome connections, occurred in the final month of the year. On the first day of December 1942, Sergeant William (Bill) Kerslake of the Royal Air Force died in Borneo. The 24-year-old was the youngest son of William John and Amelia Charlotte Kerslake of 6 Bath Street, Frome. William was educated at the County Secondary School (Frome College) – he is also one of the fourteen 'old boys' remembered on its plaque – and was a chorister at St John's Church in the town. He had joined the RAF before the war and was drafted overseas in 1939. William was based at Singapore before the fall of that port but managed to escape to Java and in February 1942 his parents received a cable from him there. In March 1943 they learned he was now a prisoner of war in Japanese hands, but by this time he had already been dead for four months. Then later in December, exactly a week before Christmas Day, Lance Bombardier Ronald George Guy Durnford also died. Before his service, Ronald was employed as a compositor by Butler & Tanner and was the president of the local branch of the Typographical Association. Ronald Durnford and William Kerslake are buried at Labuan War Cemetery in Malaysia.

As in the First World War, prisoners of war were not forgotten by the people of Frome and PoW funds had been quickly set up at the outbreak of this latest conflict. One of the organizations involved was Frome's Comforts Fund Committee, which saw to it that regular parcels were sent out to those in enemy hands, wherever they were being held, but especially at Christmas. The *Somerset Standard*, in its turn, printed throughout the war many of the letters received by the committee from men grateful not only for the contents of their parcels, which often included knitwear, but also the fact they were being thought about by the people at home.

'I wish to thank you very much for your most welcome gift, hoping you have had as much pleasure making it as I shall wearing it,' one letter began, while another wrote: 'Thank you very much for your kindness. You could not have sent a more useful gift, as socks are the one item of clothing which causes more bother than anything in Army life.' The general feeling of many was summed up by the PoW who wrote that:

I should like to express my appreciation of the gift from the above Fund. My thanks are due to the organisers, supporters and workers who made such a gift possible. It is gratifying to know that the people of Frome think of us who are away from home, and are prepared to express their thoughts in this practical manner.

The sender of the following no doubt spoke for all PoW parcel recipients when he signed off with: 'Thank you, from the bottom of my heart.'

CHAPTER SIX

The Road to D-Day: January 1943–June 1944

The year of 1943 began badly in Frome with several non-local aerial fatalities either side of the New Year. The penultimate day of the previous year had witnessed the crash of a Wellington bomber at Crastley Farm, Beckington with the loss of an airman, while four days into the new one, another Wellington came down at Orchardleigh, near Frome, causing the deaths of two more and injuring a third.

Despite these disheartening losses of life so close to home, an editorial in the first *Somerset Standard* of the New Year – topped by the headline 'This is Everyone's Battle' – was resolute that Frome should do all in its power 'to overcome the weapon by which Hitler still seeks to strangle us', the weapon in question being the German U-boat threat to the Atlantic convoys bringing vital supplies to Britain:

> 'The small islands in which we live are far from self-sufficient,' continued the editorial, '[and to] bring us many of the necessities of every-day life from across the seas, men risk death and drowning from the U-boat torpedo. Every scrap we save, every small thing we do without, reduces the number of journeys they must make, releases ships for offensive purposes. Bones, paper, metal, rubber – all these must be salvaged because many

of their sources of supply have been cut off. But they must also be salvaged so that ships will not need to brave the U-boat menace bringing them to these islands.'

In case the message had not already hit home, an example was given which pulled no punches: 'Recently a cargo vessel carrying bones to make high explosives was lost through enemy action. The men who went down with their ship might have been saved had the housewives of Britain salvaged their kitchen bones more diligently.'

One of the many 'Dig For Victory' posters issued during wartime.

Meanwhile, another piece in the same edition put the war in a wider context. Although its author admitted it was far too early to engage in any rash speculations, nevertheless,

> at least we can say that the news has never been better in the course of the war and our united arms have never, until the last two months, been more successful. In every theatre of war – on land and sea – the Germans (with their jackal followers, the Italians, the Hungarians, the Roumanians and the Bulgarians) and the Japanese, are finding themselves up against something which until the latter stages of [last] year – with several notable exceptions – they had not experienced to any serious extent – defeat!

Given the incredible effort that people within the Frome district had made to the war effort year on year, up to that point, it was unlikely they required any further remonstration to continue doing so. Therefore it was no doubt pure coincidence that a little more than a fortnight after the editorial appeared, a 'Waste Rubber Drive' organized by Frome Urban District Council

Recycling: not a present-day concept (or not in the same way).

began. The council, with the assistance of the Youth Movement, as announced in the *Somerset Standard*, would be making house-to-house collections on two consecutive Saturdays: 16 and 23 January 1943. Householders were entreated to turn out items such as old hot water bottles, hose pipes, old rubber mats and door stops, all of which were urgently needed towards the war effort. On the initial Saturday, nine teams – comprising sixty to seventy Youth Service collectors – undertook to cover the northern part of Frome, while seven teams of between forty to fifty collectors went around the lesser-populated southern half on the second one. In terms of materials, it seemed there was hardly anything that could not be 'salvaged', recycled, reused, melted down, saved or countless other processes which turned previously worthless 'rubbish' or scrap into raw material for use in the war effort. This included not only rubber but rags, bones, kitchen waste and books; another 'drive' later in the year, this time lasting for two weeks, aimed to collect 20,000 of the latter.

Possibly the most contentious 'salvage' scheme during the war was the one connected with the removal of iron railings. As Alastair MacLeay stated in an article for the Frome Society

Frome took part in numerous national campaigns, including this one for salvage.

for Local Studies' yearbook in 2012: 'Many of Frome's houses, both large and small, as well as terraced houses built before the 1930s, were embellished with iron railings [but] almost seventy years ago, at the height of the Second World War, the appearance of the town changed within a matter of weeks.' The emergency powers instigated by the government 'demanded the forfeit of "unnecessary" iron railings, gates, chains, bollards etc';

FROME YOUTH SERVICE

GUIDE

TO

YOUTH ORGANISATIONS

WHICH SHALL I JOIN ?

Issued by Frome District Youth Committee

Chairman : Rev. T. A. BAMPTON. 101, Nunney Road
Leader-Organiser : Miss A. N. PICKERING. 36, Portway
Hon. Secretaries : Mr. S. H. CRUTTWELL. 22, Bath Street
        Mr. D. W. HUMPHREYS. Innox Hill House

' Standard ' Printing, Frome

Frome Urban District Council was given assistance by the Youth Movement.

exceptions being made where removal might lead to endangering public safety, being a threat to cattle, or architecturally important. Due to the shortage of tools and supplies required for other purposes – such as oxy-acetylene torches and hacksaws – heavy hammers were used (resulting in equally heavy criticism), leaving partly-demolished walls and metal stumps poking up from the small walls they had previously adorned. The work began in early 1943 and no area of Frome was unaffected.

There has been a growing belief in recent years that the entire removal of iron railings was nothing more than a public relations exercise undertaken to make the populace feel they were contributing to the war effort; others believe the scheme began as intended, but the vast amount collected far exceeded that which could be successfully 'recycled' and so was dumped. This has perhaps been validated, as one former dock worker has claimed that much of this 'surplus' was towed down the Thames in barges and unceremoniously dumped. Whatever the truth surrounding these railings, Frome was permanently deprived of an integral part of its landscape.

One of the most badly-needed fundamentals was still, of course, money and there continued to be a seemingly never-ending number of fund-raising initiatives, such as the 'Penny-a-Week' fund and the firmly-established annual military week. This year it was titled 'Wings for Victory', with a target set of £175,000. The people of Frome once more rose to the occasion and raised £231,804 10s 2d, exceeding the target by more than £55,000.

It wasn't only money the people of Frome district were asked to 'save' in order to contribute to the war effort. Electricity became 'rationed' through the use (or rather non-use) during what were known as 'zero' hours, between 8 o'clock in the morning and 1 o'clock in the afternoon. 'Even if the temperature is at zero too,' advertisements for the scheme announced, 'don't use that electric fire – as war factories need all the power they can get during that time.'

On Friday, 12 March 1943, the ceremony for Frome District to officially 'adopt' HMS *Thunderbolt* – through the 'Exchange of Tokens' – was held at the Grand Cinema in Frome. The previous

YOUTH SERVICE ORGANISATIONS

If you want to join any of these organisations go and see Leader named below at the time and place mentioned

Name of Organisation	Place of Meeting	Days and Times of the Meeting	Leader
Brit. Red Cross Youth Det.	St. Catherine's Hall, Park Rd.	Mondays, 7.30 p.m.	Miss M. E. Davies Commandants Miss D. E. Wood
Brit. Red Cross Cadet Unit	St. Catherine's Hall, Park Rd.	Mondays, 6.30 p.m.	Miss K. Barnes, Leader
St. John Ambulance Nursing Division	St. Catherine's Hall, Park Rd.	Tuesdays, 7.30 p.m.	Miss M. A. A. Faulkner, Div. Supt.
St. John Ambulance Nursing Cadets (Girls)	Blue House, Market Place	Saturdays, 2 p.m.	Miss E. Colley, Cadet Supt.
Girls' Training Corps	Milk Street Council School	Mondays & Thursdays, 7.15—9.15 p.m.	Miss G. Udell, Commandant
Junior Girls' Training Corps	Youth Centre, Christchurch Street East	Mondays, 6.30 p.m.	Miss F. Kent, Commandant
Girls' Life Brigade	Zion Church Hall	Fridays, 6—8.30 p.m.	Miss E. K. More, Captain
Girl Guides	Holy Trinity School Hall	Saturdays, 2.30—4 p.m.	Miss Felce, Captain

Air Training Corps	Coopers' Company's School, Bath Road St. John's Senior School	Sundays, 10.30 a.m. Tuesdays and Thursdays, 7.30 p.m.	Flt.-Lt. J. A. Farnham, Officer Commanding
Army Cadet Force	A.C.F. Headquarters, Catherine Hill Drill Hall, Keyford	Tuesdays, 7.30 p.m. Fridays, 7.30 p.m.	Capt. A. E. Edwards, Officer Commanding
Civil Defence Messenger Service	Messenger Depot, Youth Centre	10–12 Nightly in rotation Training and Exercises as arranged	Mr. S. H. Cruttwell, Responsible Officer
N.F.S. Messengers	N.F.S. Station, Christchurch Street West	Alternate Sundays, 10 a.m.—12 noon	Messenger S. Newman
Police Auxiliary Messengers	Frome Police Station	As required	Police-Sergt. Sansom
St. John Ambulance Cadets (Boys)	Blue House, Market Place	Wednesdays, 7 p.m.	Mr. D. J. Moran, Cadet Sergt.
Boy Scouts	Portway Methodist Schoolroom	Fridays, 7 p.m.	Scoutmaster J. R. Standing

There were various Youth Organizations available to join within Frome.

Members of various Youth Organizations.

year, during Warship Week, the people of Frome District had raised enough money (in fact, more than enough) to 'adopt' the submarine. Since then, schoolchildren from the town had written to her crew, sending good wishes, books and magazines, and in return had received a letter from the ship's commander to say how grateful his men had been to receive the items and that

Railings at Keyford taken, along with many others in Frome, but never replaced.

FROME & DISTRICT
Wings for Victory Week—

1546

May 29—5 June, 1943

OUR TARGET:

£175,000—

For
**4 Halifax
Bombers**
and **3**
Spitfires

The annual 'military' week for 1943 was called 'Wings for Victory'.

a brass plate with their school's name had now been fixed to the ship's magnetic compass (the compass had been 'purchased' by the schoolchildren during Warship Week through a contribution of almost £400).

On entering service in the latter part of 1940, HMS *Thunderbolt* had joined the 3rd Submarine Flotilla and was

A newspaper advert showing the target to be achieved during 'Wings for Victory' week.

Frome and District "Wings for Victory" Week

FARMERS' GIFT SALE

£650 FOR A PIG ! £500 FOR GARDEN ROLLER ! !

On Wednesday, the above was held in the Market Yard. Mr. A. P. Ames and Mr. W. M. Jones having addressed the company, Mr. W. M. Jones, in a most professional and able manner, conducted, the auction sale.

Certificates were purchased to the value of £60 for a One Pound Note ; £400 for Five Guineas ; £250 for Four Pounds ; Calves from £120 to £420 ; lamb £320 ; pigs £100 to £650 each ; hens, £40 to £80 ; hen and 8 ducklings, £230 ; 1 dozen eggs £60 ; garden roller, £500.

The total raised was £7.558

One of the many fund-raising events that took place during the 'Wings for Victory' week.

D12099 (NN2 file)

WINGS FOR VICTORY WEEK
A SELECTION OF EVENTS

A 1,000 to 2,000 lb bomb (empty) was placed outside the post office in the Market Place. The people of Frome then had the opportunity of covering it with as many thickness of saving stamps as they wished, the stamp money they donated to the fund. At the end of the week the bomb with the stamps attached was filled at a munitions factory, and taken by a Halifax bomber to Germany and dropped with **FROME'S COMPLIMENTS.**

Mells held many fund raising events one of which was an Eight a side tug-of-war between a team of men and a team of woman. The men's handicap was pulling with one hand. There was great applause when the woman won.

Nunney the main attraction was boat races on Nunney brook with teams of Men, Woman and children. They also held a mock auction where large sums of money were paid for trivial items. One banana fetched £3.

Trudox Hill £25 was paid for a tin of Golden Syrup, a Calf that was auctioned three times brought in £386.

Tytherington Lots of events were arranged including a social. Where the children gave a short operetta, "Little Jessie's dream."

Outlying villages also took part in contributing to the 'Wings for Victory' week.

soon in the thick of the action during the Battle of the Atlantic. Her first 'kill' was an Italian submarine, the *Tarantini*, which she torpedoed on the morning of 15 December 1940 and by the beginning of the present year, 1943, had sunk six more ships by torpedo, another six by gun action and had served on two special assignments. By now, it seemed that apart from a single dog clip on the rear doors of each torpedo tube (universally known in the submarine service as the '*Thetis* clip') and the dirty brown high-water mark that persisted in showing through in certain compartments no matter how many coats of paint were administered, all memory of her previous identity as HMS *Thetis* and her tragic past had been erased.

It is therefore perhaps with huge irony and utmost tragedy that even as the tokens were being exchanged in the Grand Cinema on that Friday evening in March 1943, HMS *Thunderbolt* was setting out on what would be her final patrol. Having sighted a large enemy convoy in the Mediterranean, *Thunderbolt* had swiftly dispatched the largest freighter within the group to the bottom of the sea and then quickly submerged in order to escape an Italian escort ship. The commander of this latter vessel, however, had served on submarines and now used his experience to 'second guess' the movements of his adversary. Eventually *Thunderbolt* surfaced and at that moment two dozen enemy depth-charges hurtled from their racks and, for the second time in her four-year existence, the submarine sank with the loss of her entire crew.

The announcement of HMS *Thunderbolt*'s demise was made on 21 April 1943 with the words: 'The Admiralty regrets to announce that His Majesty's Submarine *Thunderbolt* must now be considered lost.' Although, as far as is known, there were no men from the Frome district on board the submarine, there were those with a Somerset connection, including 22-year-old Stoker Frederick Charles Newman of Bath.

In Frome, a memorial for the submarine and her crew would later be held at St John's Church and a fund started to help the families of those lost in the tragedy. Meanwhile, with the knowledge there was still a war to be won, Frome District councils applied to 'adopt' another warship and were allocated HMS *Montrose*. She had been launched in May 1919 and was part of the *Scott* class (so called as the ships were named after figures from Scottish history and, in this particular case, the Graham Dukes of Montrose). The ship began the Second World War on anti-submarine patrols in the Atlantic before taking part at Dunkirk – on one trip more than 900 troops were successfully evacuated by *Montrose* back to Dover – and then later escorted convoys to North Russia. Sometime during 1943, she began patrols off the coast of Britain and then in June 1944,

FROME PARISH CHURCH

❖

DEDICATION OF H.M.S. "THUNDERBOLT" MEMORIAL PLAQUE

By THE LORD BISHOP OF BATH & WELLS

❖

UNVEILING by ADMIRAL OF THE FLEET, THE EARL OF CORK & ORRERY

❖

INTRODUCTION

Brethren in the Lord : We are come to-day in order to render a solemn tribute before God and this Company in Memory of those, who in these years of war, have made the great Sacrifice In particular we honour those Officers and Men of H.M.S. " THUNDERBOLT " who gave their lives for their Country.

We are come also in order to Dedicate and Unveil a Tablet as a lasting token of our gratitude and remembrance.

It is right and fitting that we render heartfelt thanks to Almighty God for the glorious example of those whom we honour ; and that we pray for grace to render their sacrifice fruitful in the days that are ahead, whether in time of war or in time of peace.

Let us, as we stand here, lift up our hearts to our Heavenly Father and unite in saying

THE LORD'S PRAYER

The announcement of HMS Thunderbolt's dedication plaque.

HMS *Montrose* was engaged in a support role to the Normandy landings. During this action the ship was damaged and had to be towed away for repairs. These were never completed, however, and Frome's newly-adopted ship was placed on the reserve list, where she remained until the end of the war.

Around the same time Frome was 'adopting' the *Montrose*, HMS *Frome* was launched. She was a frigate of the River class, meaning she had been named for the river, not the town. Nevertheless, there was still some kind of connection for those that wanted one. The ship began her service in the Royal Navy as an anti-submarine escort and continued in this role until March the next year, when she was transferred to the Free French Naval Forces and renamed *L'Escarmouche*. From then, like the *Montrose*, the ship was primarily occupied with escorting transports and supply ships in the English Channel which, in June 1944, included the American transports heading for Utah and Omaha Beaches on D-Day.

There were no fatalities of local men during the first three months of 1943, but in April there were two. The first of these, Sergeant Arthur Wesley Frapwell, was killed in a flying accident in Yorkshire. The 22-year-old son of Wesley Alfred and Lavinia Mary Frapwell of 64 Keyford, Frome, and had been educated

HMS Montrose *was adopted by Frome, after the tragic demise of HMS* Thunderbolt.

at the Council School in the town and worked for the World's Stores before joining the RAF in February 1942. During a night-time cross-country training flight, the port engine failed on the Whitworth Whitley bomber on which he was a crew member, the pilot lost control and the aircraft crashed. Arthur's body was brought home to Frome and was buried at Christ Church, while also being remembered at Memorial Hall and Trinity Church.

Likewise, Leading Aircraftman William Albert Garrett was also a member of the Royal Air Force Volunteer Reserve and was killed in April 1943 when he was mugged and murdered in Bengal. He had been born in Corsley, but the family had

Gravestone in Frome of Sergeant Frapwell, killed in a flying accident in Yorkshire.

subsequently moved to Frome. On leaving school, he had worked in a radio shop at Church Steps, repairing and making radios, and then later driving for a local road construction firm. He joined the militia six months before war broke out and joined the RAF in 1940. He was sent to India in 1942 and had been serving there for nearly a year when he met his death, along with fifteen other servicemen. It happened on the night of 22 April 1943 after a shopping trip to a bazaar in Bengal, where they had bought items to send home. In an ambush set by a religious faction, several of the servicemen were tortured before being killed and robbed of everything they had. William was buried with full military honours and a memorial service for him was held at Corsley, attended by members of the local Home Guard.

Incredibly, apart from the deaths of Arthur Frapwell and William Garrett, there were no Frome men killed in action for almost the first six months of 1943. However, this changed on 28 June 1943, with the loss of two local men during the same bombing mission.

In early 1942, Sir Arthur Harris, immortalized as 'Bomber' Harris, had been appointed commander-in-chief of Bomber Command. Harris was a key advocate of what was known as 'strategic' bombing (as opposed to 'tactical' in support of the other two armed services) and his time in charge of Bomber Command proved to be as controversial as the type of bombing he favoured. Although no clear definition of 'strategic' bombing was ever truly established, its results were devastating. Before 1939, many experts predicted strategic bombing could, by itself, win a future war and in 1943, the RAF and US Army Air Forces (USAAF) had enough support – logistically and politically – to put the theory into practice. A combined offensive was agreed upon, whereby the USAAF would bomb industrial targets and communications by day, while the RAF would bomb enemy cities by night.

During the summer of 1943 Harris deployed the aircraft under his command to continuously attack the same targets – the vast majority being cities – over and over again. These included Berlin, Hamburg and several in the north of Germany. To begin with though, between March and July, the RAF concentrated on the Ruhr industrial area. During this campaign, several airmen from Frome took part, including the two killed on the same operation: Sergeants Dennis Coles and Jack Hole.

Dennis Coles' father was one half of Coles & Bastin Auctioneers of Frome, and the future sergeant pilot was educated at the Frome County Secondary School. On 28 June 1943, Bomber Command dispatched 608 aircraft to attack the city of Cologne. Among the aircraft were several Halifax bombers from 76 Squadron, including the one piloted by Sergeant Coles. Although the target was cloud-covered and around half the intended markers were not dropped, the raid was deemed a 'success' and became the worst suffered by Cologne during the war. However, twenty-five aircraft were lost in the raid, including the one flown by Sergeant Coles. The plane crashed, most likely due to being shot down by a night-fighter, and the seven-man crew died.

Sergeant Jack Gordon Hole was the son of George and Catherine Hole of Frome and was attached to 467 Squadron, Royal Australian Air Force. At the time of the mission, the squadron was equipped with Lancaster bombers and Sergeant Hole was a rear gunner in one of these. At 2251 hours on the 28th (around ninety minutes later than Sergeant Coles' Halifax), Sergeant Hole's Lancaster took to the skies. During the operation it too was shot down by a night-fighter over Holland and crashed at 01.30 am. There were two survivors but sadly Sergeant Jack Hole was not one of them.

December 1943 saw the completion of the notorious Burma-Siam railway – intended to improve communications for the Japanese army – but which, during its fourteen-month construction, claimed the lives of approximately 13,000 Commonwealth, Dutch and American prisoners of war. Two labour forces, one in Siam, the other in Burma, worked from opposite ends of the 424 kilometre-long line towards the centre.

The graves of those PoWs who died during the construction and maintenance of the Burma-Siam railway (except for Americans, whose remains were repatriated) were transferred from camp burial grounds and isolated sites along the railway into three cemeteries at Chungkai and Kanchanaburi in Siam (latter-day Thailand) and Thanbyuzayat in Burma (now Myanmar).

One of the men who died working on the construction of the railway and is buried at Chungkai War Cemetery was 23-year-old George Francis Garnett of the Royal Corps of Signals. He had been employed before the war at the Frome Post Office on counter duty and was first reported missing in action in Malaya on 27 March 1942. He is reported as having died on 18 August 1943 and is remembered at the Memorial Hall.

October 1943 saw two more deaths of Frome PoWs; this time working on opposite ends of the railway. On the third day of the month Private Cecil Robert Huggard of the Royal Army Ordnance Corps died. He was 29 years old and is buried at Thanbyuzayat War Cemetery and remembered on the memorial at Rode. Meanwhile, at the other end of the month on 30 October 1943 and working on the other end of the railway (from Siam) when he died of the tropical disease beriberi, was Leslie James Burge. The second son of Mr and Mrs Arthur J. Burge of Horton Street, Frome, he had been educated at St John's Boys' School and been employed at the Frome United Breweries before the war. He was serving with the Royal Artillery when captured, being among the 60,000 British servicemen taken prisoner when General Percival surrendered the island of Singapore to the Japanese on 15 February 1942.

His wife Muriel received the following letter from her husband's battery commander:

> You will have been notified by now by the War Office that your husband unhappily lost his life whilst a prisoner of war in Japanese hands and I am writing to express my very deep sympathy with you. He was a splendid chap and a fine soldier and I was proud to have him under my command. He is buried in the beautifully arranged cemetery in Chungkai in Siam with others of his comrades who lost their lives in the same way.

However, not all Frome PoWs who lost their lives during the war died on the infamous railway line. Like his namesake Donald Godfrey Heath who had died in November 1942, Aircraftman 2nd Class Reginald Arthur Heath has no known grave. Unlike Donald, who died on land, Reginald died at sea. Husband of Lillian Sarah Heath of 6 The Lays, Fromefield, Frome, he had joined the RAF in 1941 and became attached to 605 Squadron, Royal Air Force Volunteer Reserve, which was on its way to Singapore. However, it arrived too late to contribute to the defence of Singapore and was evacuated to Sumatra. From there they moved on to Java and it was here he was taken prisoner by the Japanese in March 1942. Records show that from Java he was transferred to the Indonesian island of Ambon but then, in November 1943, had been put aboard a ship, the *Suez Maru*, to be transported back to Java along with more than 500 PoWs, most of whom were considered too weak to work. The ship was attacked by American submarine USS *Bonefish* and sunk on 29 November 1943. All PoWs died on board, drowned or were callously and mercilessly machine-gunned or rammed while still in the water by the Japanese navy.

For most servicemen from Frome away from home, hopes of returning to the town, even on a short-leave pass, no doubt occupied much of their thoughts and perhaps even their nightly dreams, but for one soldier the reality of a return turned out to be a nightmare. His post-visit letter, addressed to the editor, appeared in the *Somerset Standard* earlier in the year and was headed 'Social Amenities for Troops on Leave':

> 'Sir – Having recently visited Frome,' it began, 'I am particularly distressed with the apparent lack of social amenities for the troops on leave in the district. After nearly a year spent under trying conditions...I am asking myself, "Why did I come home to such a sleepy town?" Frome boasts of two cinema programmes and possibly two dances per week. To look for further entertainment is surely an abortive task. As to our dance-halls – I have to ask, "Where are they?" Three in number seem to hit the headlines in

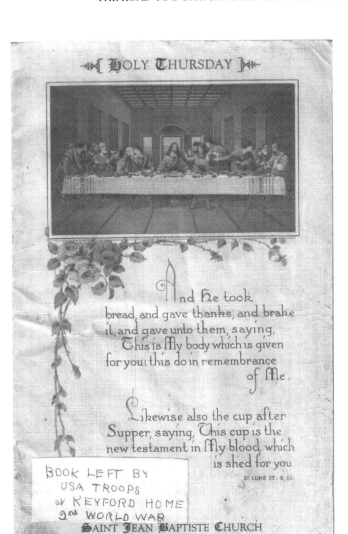

One of the items left behind by American GIs who came to Frome.

our local paper: The George Hotel, The Co-operative Hall and The Drill Hall. We have a good floor to dance on at the first-mentioned ballroom, but no room to dance. At the two latter, a dance resembles a Tommy Farr-Max Bear fight at the Empire Stadium.... For the Servicemen on leave in Frome, the forenoon and afternoon hours constitute a continuous bore of wandering aimlessly around our streets

An invitation to a dance at Frome Drill Hall being held by the Coldstream Guards.

trying to occupy time. Where is the lovely little café we find in so many of our towns? You know, the ones with a radio...in the corner, where one can have morning coffee or afternoon tea to the latest tune. So, Frome, how about it? How about some entertainment for the troops on leave? Your own sons and daughters in particular!'

The letter was signed 'A DISGUSTED F/SGT.' Perhaps not unexpectedly, it generated a mountain of replies and also compelled the editor of the *Somerset Standard* to write a leader entitled 'Poor old Frome!!!' In the piece, the editor defended Frome and its people, including a well-placed observation that there seemed to be an inference on the part of the 'Disgusted Flight Sergeant' and those who had subsequently written to agree with his tirade that they were the only ones 'doing their bit'. However, the truth, as the editor pointed out, was that

while those home on leave are seeking someone to amuse them, these people are fire-watching, or doing some form of A.R.P work, serving at canteens etc., many of [whom]

have had little or no holidays since the commencement
of the war and are still carrying on, with no thought of
defeat or complaint.

As for the fellow soldiers who wrote in, not all were on the same
wavelength as 'Disgusted'. The feeling and sentiment of the
majority of them was summed up by a letter signed 'A Happy
Trooper' in which he bluntly said:

> May I say that he does not realise how well off he is, as
> he says 'Frome is enough to drive anyone to drink, for
> there are only 2 cinemas, 3 dance halls, 1 public park and
> swimming bath', and that none of the cafés were suitable
> for him. May I ask what more he wants? [and there] are
> thousands of chaps out here who would change places
> with 'Disgusted'. [At the same time] I come from Bath
> and have always found the people of Frome to be kind-
> hearted and good-natured.

The City of Bath (along with Trowbridge) had also been
mentioned in regard to them being places rather than Frome
where servicemen preferred to travel in order to enjoy their
leave, but the *Somerset Standard* editor had a rebuke for this
as well. On a recent trip to Bath, he had been waiting at its
railway station when a train arrived from nearby Bristol, full
of Bath people who had gone to the larger city in order to find
amusement. As for Trowbridge, while on the journey home,
he had got into a conversation with a fellow traveller who
announced that 'It was a treat to get out of Trowbridge, as it
was "the last place God made".'

There were no doubt servicemen on either side of the
argument, probably even locals, but the reality is there were
numerous avenues of entertainment in the town that existed for
everyone. Perhaps the most dominant source of entertainment,
certainly in households, factories and army quarters, although
seemingly not in the town's cafés, was the wireless or radio.
Not only was it the prime source of news and information

regarding the war through the BBC Home Service, but also the light entertainment service which broadcast such programmes as *ITMA* (*It's That Man Again*), *Children's Hour* and *Workers' Playtime*. Evans Engineering, of course, had had several lunchtime broadcasts on the latter, as well as *Works Wonders* concerts. Along with public services, there was also the Forces Programme radio station providing a twelve-hour daily dose of entertainment for the troops; this had begun back in 1940.

Another very popular radio show was, *Music While You Work*. Often the role played by music in keeping morale high is understated. There is no doubt such songs as *We'll Meet Again*, *The White Cliffs of Dover*, *Run Rabbit Run* and *(We're Gonna Hang Out) The Washing on the Siegfried Line* played their own important part in the war effort, but it wasn't just the recorded versions, made famous by Vera Lynn and Flanagan and Allen respectively, kept spirits boosted and ultimately helped in the winning of the war, but also the singing of the songs themselves, for example in groups gathered around a pub piano on a Saturday night in the pubs and inns of the Frome area, which cemented unity and the community spirit and reinforced the feeling that 'We're all in this together.'

If the thought of a pub sing-a-long was not your cup of tea though, there were other options open to the populace of Frome as well as those on home leave. One of these, as mentioned in the flurry of correspondence, was the cinema. Despite Frome being the location for two of them – the Gaumont and the Grand – this was seemingly not good enough for those who wrote 'against' Frome's amenities, and yet both of them, as the *Somerset Standard* pointed out in its editorial piece, presented programmes which were 'comparable in quality with those furnished by any town of a similar size'. These included, during the war years, patriotic films such as *In Which We Serve* – 'starring' one of Frome's own Notts' Carley floats – mixed with popular romantic films such as *Brief Encounter*, Hollywood epics such as *Gone with the Wind*, comedies like *Champagne Charlie* starring Tommy Trinder and Stanley Holloway, and George Formby's *He Snoops to Conquer*, and future classics such as *The Wizard of Oz* and *Casablanca*.

There had been a nationwide closure of cinemas, including those in Frome, at the outbreak of war – the government's fear being that large numbers of people gathered together under one roof might lead to massive loss of life from the expected bombing raids – but they soon reopened when these attacks failed to materialize. This was no doubt a huge relief to all those people who would, during the war years, buy between 25 and 30 million tickets a week as they sought out the latest films that would provide escapism from the realities of life for a few hours.

If people preferred 'real life' to mere celluloid representations, Frome theatre-goers were more than amply catered for throughout the war by various performances. The town had several venues able to accommodate performances and these were put to good use by a number of repertory groups. One of these was the Coopers' Company's School Dramatic Society and an early production by them was *Judgement Day* by American playwright Elmer Rice, which was performed at the Grand Cinema in February 1940. Some 500 locals who were billeting Coopers' Company's staff and boys were invited to the performance free of charge as a mark of appreciation by the school, while the profits from the remaining tickets that went on sale were given to the Frome branch of the WVS. Other productions included *Toad of Toad Hall*, *A Midsummer Night's Dream* and *The Importance of Being Earnest*. At the same time, plays written by boys from Coopers' Company's School were produced, to notable acclaim by the local paper in one case. '*Murder in the Study* was perhaps the high spot of the evening,' exclaimed the *Somerset Standard* in March 1944, 'a truly riotous farce, a burlesque on Sherlock Holmes. Cpl Wingfield, ATC, was the author of this laughable little melodrama and he is to be warmly congratulated.'

The author of the play, Corporal Rodney D. Wingfield, would later find fame as the creator of the *Frost* novels, which were adapted for television as *A Touch of Frost* and starred David Jason in the title role of Jack Frost. Rodney was not the only boy from the school to become a noteworthy alumnus within 'the arts'. At the same time at the school and no doubt acting in many of its productions was a boy called Monty Goldberg. He would later become the well-known actor Lee Montague, winning national recognition as one of the best actors of his generation. Another boy, Norman Cranwell, also became a professional actor after the war.

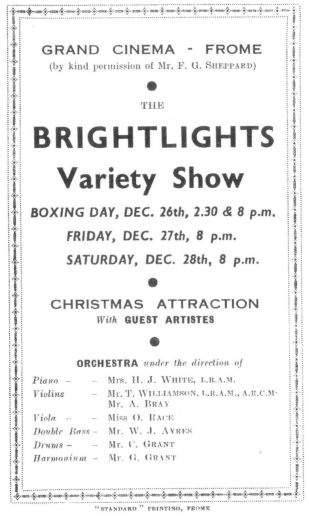

A trio of variety shows played by 'The Bright Lights', formed by members of Frome.

If variety was what you were after though, then this 'spice of life' was provided by a 'home-grown' company who provided continuous entertainment throughout the entire war years. In September 1939, Frome Operatic Society ceased its operations and its members decided to form a concert party called 'The Bright Lights'. A typical programme included 'sketches', 'musical frolics' and 'dancing', along with various 'solo and duet numbers'. Along with many performances at the Grand Cinema, they also entertained troops stationed in the surrounding areas, and often played to audiences comprising as many as 2,000 soldiers. All the members of the company had daytime jobs – the majority also held civil defence roles – and so had to fit in rehearsals, shows and travelling around their work and other obligations. When performing outside of the town, facilities for changing were rudimentary at best and non-existent at worst (apparently at one show an army blanket had to be secured in order to give the female cast members a modicum of privacy). Nevertheless, 'The Bright Lights' successfully performed hundreds of shows during the war, raised much-needed monies for charities associated with the war effort and no doubt brought much-needed entertainment to the public and armed services alike. From 1943 onwards, the latter included an influx of ever-increasing numbers of American soldiers.

'Got any gum, chum?' and 'Overpaid, oversexed and over here' seem to be the two phrases that must emanate from locals' lips when questioned about the American GIs in Frome during wartime. The first, predominately asked by schoolboys on seeing any American soldiers who began to arrive in the area throughout the latter part of 1943, was usually answered with a reciprocal 'Yeah, got any sisters?'; the reply going a long way to confirm the validity of the second phrase, i.e. the middle part, that of being 'oversexed'.

These phrases, as audibly pleasing as they are sardonically true, nevertheless seem to condense the period when American soldiers were based in the area to a set of almost rose-tinted and oft-repeated phrases and sayings belying the fact it was actually one of the most inflammatory, racially explosive and, as we shall see, murderously violent periods in the entire history of the town; and given Given Frome's notorious and riotous past throughout the centuries, that is saying a lot!

America entered the Second World War on 7 December 1941 following the Japanese attack on Pearl Harbor, and by the following month her troops had arrived upon British soil. The build-up of US forces continued unabated through early 1942, in support of a proposed invasion of France later that year or the next but was halted over concerns such an attack would be premature. In the second half of 1943, however, the build-up of American forces in Britain resumed in earnest as Operation NEPTUNE (the Normandy landings leading to D-Day) began to be counted down (and at its peak there would be 1,600,000 American service personnel stationed within Great Britain). Huge areas of southern England became divided into two areas: Concentration and Marshalling. Frome was part of the first, along with the rest of Somerset, and until the movement of troops to the marshalling areas began in May 1944, large numbers of American GIs were stationed in Frome and the surrounding areas, with a substantial number still in the town as late as 1945.

Among the places requisitioned as billets in the area were Marston House and Orchardleigh, the officers having their quarters inside the main houses, while their men set up 'camp' in the grounds and wooded areas on the rest of the estates. Hotels – as previously used by the British 130 Brigade and then Montgomery's 3rd Division – also became temporary residences of the Americans, along with numerous other buildings, offices, houses and functional sites.

Aside from their gum, glamour, attitude, money, nylons, chocolate and countless other attributes which made them instantly attractive to certain sections of the local population, the presence of the American soldiers in Frome, as elsewhere, brought with it a huge set of problems; the two most inflammatory ones being those of sex and race. For if sexual relations between the white American GIs and local women had the potential to arouse emotions – among British soldiers stationed nearby and other male members of the community – it was nothing in comparison to the situation when black American GIs were added to the mix.

The British government had tried to persuade their American ally not to send black soldiers to Britain during the build-up to D-Day – perhaps rightly foreseeing the problems that would arise – but was overridden. In an effort to try to at least lessen the effects of this influx, the government then introduced a series of restrictive measures: particular towns became off limits to one or other of the races – the result, however, being the curtailing of leave opportunities for blacks *and* whites – while other places came under the 'alternate-day' system. This meant white American GIs could only go into these specified towns for recreational purposes on certain pre-designated nights, while their black counterparts could only go in on the alternate ones.

Frome came under the latter system – that of an alternate-day town – but any hopes of this enforced segregation putting a stop to potential racial problems failed miserably; at least according to locals who witnessed the huge fights between the black and white GIs in the Market Place, which were only usually brought to an end when fire hoses were turned on the participants and American Military Police intervened to break them up. Then there were the murders. According to the recollections of one schoolboy-turned-police-messenger, recalled years later, there were at least five racially-motivated killings within the area during that period; the first apparently discovered during the blackout by the schoolboy messenger and a local constable on their way up Bath Street to the police station. Laid out in the road, with his throat cut, was the body of a black American GI. It was reported to the American military who not long afterwards came and took the deceased soldier's body away. Another of these 'killings' took place outside the building that nowadays houses the Frome Museum. In this particular instance, the black soldier had been murdered by white GIs hailing from one of the southern American states, and then 'pinned' by knives to one of the twin doors that fronts the unusually-shaped construction.

These incidents do, of course, rely solely on oral sources as no documented evidence has been found during research for this book to authenticate these horrific incidents. However, elsewhere in the country during this period there were countless episodes of racially-motivated violence, with many resulting in fatalities, including in Bristol, Chipping Norton, Leicester, Launceston, Bamber Bridge in Lancashire and Antrim in Northern Ireland. All of these *have* been well-documented and subsequently became part of the 'official record', so to speak. Therefore, there is no reason not to accept that these incidents *could* have occurred in Frome, however awful it might be to think of them having actually happened within this town.

If Frome was an 'alternate' town in terms of stationed American GIs and their recreational passes, there was also an 'alternate' experience to the area for soldiers based here, other than the dark, violent undercurrent which seemingly prevailed. One example of this 'alternate' experience can be found in the reminiscences of a former American GI stationed at Marston House (and which first appeared in issues of the Frome Society for Local Studies yearbooks). Private Gérald Laurent LaRoche of the 472nd Replacement Company, 94th Replacement Battalion, arrived at Frome railway station in February 1944 and was taken from there, by US army truck, to his 'temporary' residence at Marston House, a few miles outside Frome centre. In the three or so months he was based in the area, his leisure time consisted mainly of visiting nearby places of cultural and architectural importance and interest, including Nunney, Bath and Frome itself, sketching many of the buildings he encountered during these trips, strolling in nearby Marston Woods, reading widely and 'carrying on' a voluminous correspondence with a legion of patriotic letter-writers from as far away as San Francisco and Montreal'. His favourite place to visit became the City of Bath and according to his own account: 'I must have walked dozens of miles exploring the terraced rows of town houses, the Roman Baths and the Pump Room, the Parade Gardens and Pulteney Bridge.' This became such a 'dream post' for him, as he later recalled, that by 'the end of a second enjoyable week I had almost forgotten why I had been sent to England in the first place.'

)12099

We're rolling 'em up!
– roll up with your Savings

Here's to the British Soldier . . . Tommy . . . who took it on the chin—and came back for more . . . who is now avenging Dunkirk, Crete, Singapore, Hong Kong. Let's Salute him. Not in words . . . but deeds . . . by making SALUTE THE SOLDIER WEEK our greatest savings triumph yet. It won't be easy. Our local savings target is high. But we can do it . . . must do it . . . by saving hard . . . all along the line . . . to make our Salute worthy of the Soldier.

SALUTE THE SOLDIER WEEK

INVEST ALL YOU CAN IN—

3% Savings Bonds 1960-70 • 2½% National War Bonds 1951-4 • 3% Defence Bonds • Savings Certificates • Savings Stamps • The Post Office Savings Bank • A Trustee Savings Bank

JUNE 10th - 17th

FROME & DISTRICT
OBJECTIVE £175,000

A newspaper 'advert' announcing 'Salute the Soldier' week in 1944.

'' (A)

‚DDARD

ary " (H)

"Certificate of the
ed, whether accom-

)OKS in

GER " (A)

‚ MARSHALL

:NG " (A)

‚SON in

'' (A)

r and Austin Saloons
‚, Station Work, etc.—
‚, Frome. 'Phone 2492.

oung Farmers' Club
‚nded that their year-
Frome Market Yard on
‚y 10th, by 11 a.m.

week Fund
‚l amounted to £111 6s.
‚ustomers at the Griffen

g Day
‚y will be held on Satur-
‚ing our readers for their
‚ past, Mrs. H. J. Green
‚d support of this worthy

o Mr. and Mrs. Lindsay,
‚ne, Frome, who on Sun-
‚h, celebrated their 55th
‚y. Although Mr. Lind-
‚valid for some years, his
‚nd hearty," and both are
‚ their Diamond Wedding
‚ent which occurred in
‚ Lindsay's parents, the
‚ Crocker, of the Flints,

Hospital
‚l like to take this oppor-
‚ the following friends for
‚pport and help :—Mrs.
‚flowers ; Mrs. Bridge,
‚erproof sheets ; Major
‚:s ; Mrs. Gardener, cauli-
‚w, leeks ; Mrs. Anstey,
‚uddick, rhubarb ; Mrs.
‚ls ; Janet Truddick,
‚eman, tin-foil.
‚vegetables and rhubarb
‚ceptable for the use of
‚t the Hospital.

niversary
‚vn Mission anniversary
‚was held in Bethel Chapel
‚e occasion), on Monday
‚. R. Jenkins (President
‚sided over a large attend-
‚endid tribute to the work
‚er (Mrs. Brewer) and her
‚. A. Paterson gave an
‚his subject being, " The
‚Mrs. J. A. Farnham sang
‚Lord and Father of man-
‚‚ as a Bird." The choir
‚ " The lovely Flowers."
‚animents were shared by
‚d Miss D. Whatley. The
‚anked her large band of
‚rishes to thank all friends
‚it so many lovely flowers,

says : "' Ginger ' Jack House (trumpet) :
Bids fair to be ' The Boogie Woogie Trum-
peter of '43,' also started musical career
at age of 15—joined home town military
band : went under the able tuition of the
band leader and played second cornet.
Within two years was up among the first
men—says they never could find out what
was wrong with the band after that. Then
' Ginger ' bought a trumpet and with
enthusiastic plans, formed a small outfit
and called it ' The Equatorians '—says no
one knew why they called it that. ' Equatorians ' are still going strong to-day as
an eight-piece outfit. War, as usual,
mucked up plans. Ginger played in dance
band on training camp somewhere in England. (happy days)."

Whist Drive for Hospital Maternity Ward
An enjoyable evening was spent at the
Co-operative Hall whist drive in aid of the
Frome Victoria Hospital Maternity Ward
on Wednesday evening. Mr. Hall was M.C.,
and the prize-winners were :—Ladies : 1,
Mrs. George ; 2, Mrs. Evemy ; 3, Mrs.
White. Gents : 1, Mrs. Targett (as gent) ;
2, Mr. Hall ; 3, Miss Cox (as gent). Lucky
gifts. Mrs. Minty, Mrs. Millar, Mrs. Watts
and Mrs. Harrison. The prizes were presented by Mrs. Faulkner.

Our 'Phone No. is 2379

FROME YOUTH CRICKET CLUB

ANNUAL GENERAL MEETING

The Youth Cricket Club's annual general meeting,
was held in the Youth Centre on Monday. Mr. D.
Scott presided and the annual report for the season
was presented by the secretary, treasurer and
captain, Mr. R. Stannard, and read as folows :—
After the successful beginning of the Youth
Football Club, there was a strong call to introduce
a Frome Youth Cricket Club, to be run on the same
lines as the Football Club. Therefore, at a meeting on the 23rd of March, 1943, held in the Youth
Centre, under the able Presidency of Mr. Don
Scott, it was unanimously decided that a Club
should be formed. As Mr. Scott pointed out,

As a support, Kerry Baker appears in
BOYS IN IRELAND."

TO THE EDITOR

THANKS TO RED CROSS WORKERS

Sir,—Through the medium of your columns I
would like, on behalf of my committee, to pay a
tribute to the Red Cross Penny-a-week collectors
in Frome for their untiring service to such a great
cause. The collectors number no less than eighty-
two and devote many hours every week to this
important work.
Some complain that they are asked by subscribers whether they receive payment or commission on their collections, and I take this opportunity of assuring anyone in doubt that this is not
so. The whole of the Red Cross Penny-a-week
organisation in Frome is entirely voluntary and
every penny subscribed is handed to the Central
Fund.
Upon the basis of subscriptions per head of
population. Somerset occupies the exalted position
of 6th among the counties of England and Wales,
and in Somerset, our town of Frome (Urban) is
within the first three.
To retain our position the committee looks to the
collectors, and to improve it, to the public. Please,
therefore, continue your weekly subscription,
even if you cannot increase it, and help the Red
Cross to continue their wonderful work.

E. M. YATES,
Hon. Secretary.
" Quernmore," Rodden Road, Frome.
2nd May, 1944.

In Exile

The Frome War Savings Association is using
its organisation through its Group Collectors to
collect games and books throughout Frome and
its surrounding villages for forwarding to
prisoners of war.

INSIDE the wire of the Stalag he stands
Bitterly gazing out West ;
Grimly recalling the marching—the bands—
The leg-pulling—cheers—and the rest.

" God ! what a change ! What a life ! What a
hope !
Frustration, idleness, sloth ;

Advert for one of the events taking place during ' Salute the Soldier ' week.

That reason, of course, was the build-up towards D-Day – the invasion of Normandy and the opening up of the Second Front in the war against Hitler – and all too soon Private LaRoche's somewhat 'idyllic' existence came to an end; although not before he had met a local girl, Joyce, at a nearby dance; she would later become his wife:

On May 27th, a Saturday, all local passes off post were cancelled and the pace of troop movement preparations quickened. I could not even get to Frome to send a telegram to Joyce telling her I was unable to see her as intended. On the weekend of June 4th we were confined to our immediate company area and were told to stay close to our barracks. The next afternoon we sensed something was afoot when we saw scores of gliders being towed over Marston itself. At noon on the 6th of June we were told the Allies had invaded Normandy that morning and that our forces had secured a sizable foothold on the beaches. Two days later our entire replacement company was loaded onto a troop train that was switched in Radstock from a local line to the main Dorset line. During this operation many Yanks on board emptied their pockets of chocolate, chewing gum and British pennies as a parting gift to the dozens of youngsters who had invaded the station area. We arrived in Dorchester late during the night where we billeted in temporary quarters until it was time to cross the English Channel.

CHAPTER SEVEN

From D-Day to VJ Day: June 1944–August 1945

It is no secret the Allied invasion of Europe – D-Day – came at a heavy cost and the price paid was mainly in human life. It is perhaps no great surprise, therefore, to learn that there were more men from Frome and the surrounding areas killed during June 1944 than the total number of fatalities in the rest of the year, up until the point troops embarked for the Normandy beaches, added together. Nevertheless, their supreme sacrifice, like thousands of others, allowed a Second Front to be created and ultimately led to the Allied victory in Europe in May 1945.

If there was any strong connection between Frome and one specific army regiment, then it was the Somerset Light Infantry. Men from the town had served in the 'Somersets' since its formation back in 1685, when James II expanded the size of the army in order to quash the Monmouth Rebellion, and had fought in all subsequent conflicts that graced its battle honours. Certain battalions of the regiment had been in the thick of the action throughout most of the First World War, but the entire regiment had experienced a relatively 'quiet' and frustrating present one until this point; the two regular battalions had been in India and Gibraltar, while the remainder, stationed in England, were initially engaged in coastal defence duties and then, after Hitler abandoned his plans for invasion, constant training. Their time, however, at least for two of the battalions, was about to come.

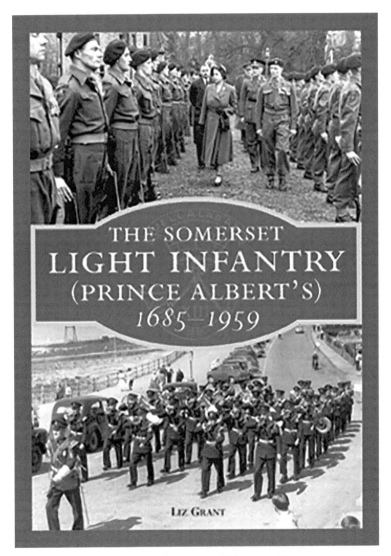

The Somerset Light Infantry had a long and illustrious history.

In June 1944, the 4th and 7th battalions of the Somerset Light Infantry were part of the 43rd (Wessex) Division, which itself formed part of VIII Corps. VIII Corps had been established in summer 1940 to control the fighting in the West Country had the Germans successfully managed to land there. By the time of D-Day, however, it had been assigned a 'follow-up' role and once in Normandy, having landed there near the end of June 1944, became part of the Second Army along with both the 11th (Armoured) and 15th (Scottish) divisions.

From the moment the 43rd Division landed upon French soil, they were called on to take a leading role in every major operation launched by the Second Army from June 1944 to May 1945 including the Battle of Caen, along with the bitterly-contested fight for Hill 112; the assault of Mont Pinçon; the first assault crossing of the Seine at Vernon; the drive into Holland and relief

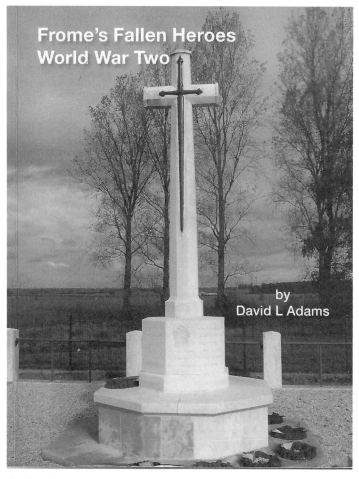

David Adams' exhaustively researched book.

of the Airborne Army at Arnhem; the Anglo-American offensive at Geilenkirchen; the clearing of the Roer Salient; the Battle of the Rhineland, culminating in the breaking of the German defences before the key town of Goch and the capture of Xanten; the Rhine Crossing and the subsequent break-out northwards; and finally, the assault and capture of Bremen.

Within that incredible battle record, however, are the individual stories of the men who died during those battles, operations and crossings, many of them from Frome or the surrounding areas. There are too many to list and not enough space to completely do justice to their sacrifice, but the reader is first directed to the Afterword at the end of this book and then, for a fuller account of the fatalities from the area, to David L. Adams' exhaustive work which chronicles those men who gave their lives during the Second World War.

June 1944 also saw the first anniversary of the opening of a British Restaurant in Frome. British Restaurants – originally called 'Community Feeding Centres' – had been set up by the Ministry of Food in 1940 and were to be run on a non-profit basis by local government or voluntary organizations. The purpose of these communal kitchens was to provide inexpensive meals (at a maximum price of 9d) to people who had been bombed out of their houses, run out of ration coupons or otherwise merely needed help in obtaining a nutritious square meal.

The resolution to establish a British Restaurant within the town had been adopted by Frome Urban District Council as far back as late 1941, but the subsequent eighteen months had seen numerous hitches, setbacks and red tape. The distinct possibility of one at St John's School had ultimately fallen through, while an alternative solution elsewhere in the shape of a Nissen hut had failed to materialize, despite Frome's MP Mavis Tate raising the matter in the House of Commons. Eventually, what is today Cork Street car park was rubber-stamped as the site and 22 June 1943 witnessed the town's very own British Restaurant, opened by the chairman of the council, H.M. Scott.

The new restaurant – which could cater for 200 people at a time – was called the 'Union Jack', the name having been

"UNION JACK"
BRITISH
RESTAURANT

♦

JUNE 22nd, 1943

OFFICIAL OPENING

BY

COUNCILLOR H. M. SCOTT, J.P.
Chairman
Frome Urban District Council

SUPPORTED BY

COUNCILLOR F. MILTON RUSS, J.P.
Vice-Chairman

AND

MEMBERS OF THE COUNCIL

The official opening of Frome's British Restaurant took place on 22 June 1943.

chosen from all those sent to the FUDC through a competition in the *Somerset Standard*. The winning name had been submitted by Miss E.A. Seward and her prize – as well as seeing her suggestion adopted – was six free lunches or twelve free teas. Other suggestions had included 'Aldhelm's Kitchen', 'West End Restaurant' and 'Selwood Snacks'. 'The Union Jack' restaurant itself was a success from the very outset and by the time of its

Menu.

Roast Beef, Churchill
Pudding, Yorkshire

———

Roast and Boiled Potatoes
Woolton

Spring Cabbage
Somerset

———

Cold Meat and Salad
Boiled Potatoes

———

Sultana Victory Roll
Custard Sauce

———

Blancmange Royal

———

Creamed Rice and Prunes

———

Biscuits and Cheese

———

Coffee

The menu at the opening of the 'Union Jack', the winning name of the British Restaurant.

anniversary twelve months later, a total of 129,514 dinners and 179,857 hot beverages had been served.

Although it seemed as if the tide was turning in favour of the Allies during the remainder of 1944, Hitler was determined to strike back and this took the form of the V-1 flying bomb and later the V-2 rocket, both of which were launched from sites in Germany to rain down terror on south-east England. One consequence of these new weapons was another mass evacuation of schoolchildren in the potentially affected areas, some of whom had actually been evacuated to their present locations which had previously been deemed 'safe havens' in 1940.

One of the schools evacuated during what became known as the Third Great Trek was Colfe's Grammar School from Lewisham. During Operation PIED PIPER back in 1940, they had been evacuated to Tunbridge Wells, but when this came in range of the V-1s or 'doodlebugs', they were moved once again. This time it was to Frome and the entire school arrived in the town in June 1944, although things did not go smoothly for some of the evacuees:

'Being wartime, people had to reveal whether they had spare space and had to accept whomever the officials brought along,' one former Colfe schoolboy later remembered. 'This led to great misery for some boys who were totally mismatched with their hosts [and at the same time the] process of billeting took a long time and some boys slept in local halls for days before being allocated.'

The school itself relocated to the Frome County School, where it shared wooden hutted 'classrooms' that had been constructed during the 1914–18 war. The unheated huts – some windowless – apparently became so cold throughout the winter months it was almost impossible to write and the boys had to keep on all their outdoor clothing as a matter of course. They remained in the town for the rest of the war and returned to Lewisham in the summer of 1945.

As the Allied forces made their way across the various theatres of war, the threat to Somerset slowly receded and then stopped. So, with the lifting of this threat, 'stand-down' parades began to occur throughout the county on a regular basis. The 4th Somerset (Frome) Battalion Home Guard held theirs on 3 December 1944, with a strength of 2,468 officers and men and 112 women auxiliaries (females had initially not been allowed to join the Home Guard, but concessions had been made and so they were designated 'auxiliaries', although not connected to the British

Special Order of the Day to the Home Guard

by

General Sir Harold E. Franklyn, K.C.B., D.S.O., M.C., Commander-in-Chief, Home Forces

GENERAL HEADQUARTERS,
HOME FORCES.

November, 1944.

During the past few years I have had many opportunities of seeing the Home Guard in most parts of the country, including Northern Ireland. A high standard of efficiency has been reached, which has been made possible only by the keenness and devotion to duty of all ranks. I would like to emphasise the very special contribution of those who volunteered in 1940 and whose enthusiasm has never flagged since then ; they have been the backbone of their units.

The Home Guard came into being at a time of acute crisis in our history, and for over four years has stood prepared to repel any invader of our shores. The reliance that has been placed on you during these years has been abundantly justified and it has enabled our Regular troops to go overseas in sufficient numbers to give battle to the enemy with the magnificent results that we have seen.

And now as to the future. I hope that Home Guardsmen will take every opportunity of preserving the friendships and associations that you have formed during these past years. You can continue to be a real source of stability and strength to the country during what may be difficult years ahead. I hope also that you will do all in your power to help the Cadets, even if only by encouragement. Here is a way in which you can continue to render valuable service for many years to come.

I am very proud to have had the Home Guard under my command. I have enjoyed meeting and speaking to thousands of you. Now you can stand down with every right to feel that you have done your duty and contributed very materially to victory.

The best of luck to every one of you.

Well done indeed the Home Guard.

General.

On stand down, General Sir Harold Franklyn sent this congratulatory message to those under his command. (CRO)

This congratulatory message was sent to members of Frome's Home Guard on the occasion of their stand-down in December 1944.

Resistance Organisation Auxiliaries in any way). A little later, on 10 May 1945, two days after VE (Victory in Europe) Day, the Royal Observer Corps likewise held their own stand-down ceremony.

Each winter of the war had seemed to be colder than the one before, and whether this was in fact true, the Christmas period of 1944 was officially one of the coldest on record. Although not actually a white Christmas, a lacework of ice had spread over trees and covered telegraph and aerial wires with needles of dazzling frost and produced as white a Christmas as if there had been a snowstorm.

Traditional dances 'saw in' 1945 and despite the Germans' last desperate attempt to turn back the tide of the war in their favour, most people believed this would be the last wartime New Year's Day and an Allied victory would be secured in the next twelve months. The sub-zero temperatures remained throughout January to the point where it was being compared to the notorious winter of 1892, which elderly residents of Frome could remember vividly.

As Europe was gradually liberated, the horrors that had taken place under German occupation began to fully reveal themselves and perhaps none more horrific than the sights which greeted Allied troops as they came across concentration camps, first in Poland and then Germany. Two of the initial camps to be 'liberated' were at Belsen and Buchenwald. As soon as Churchill and the British government were informed of the atrocities discovered by American soldiers, a delegation of British MPs was quickly gathered together to travel to the camps; among them, and the only female MP in the party, was Frome's Mavis Tate. In fact, on footage from the camps that would shock people around the world, it is she who 'presents' it.

One schoolboy who actually saw the newsreel film of the footage in Frome later recounted the reaction of the audience; one shared, no doubt, by the majority of people who saw it in the first few months of 1945:

> Most newsreels in the cinema, which showed events from the fronts were about ten minutes long, fifteen

at the most, and served as an interval between the two films on show. People clapped and cheered when, say, a U-boat was sunk or when German soldiers surrendered, but this record of what liberating armies found in Belsen and Buchenwald was long and seen in silence. We could scarcely believe our eyes. Here were emaciated bodies in heaps or in pits, some just alive, most dead. I was numbed. The events were beyond our imaginations.

As well as 'presenting' the footage of the concentration camps, Mavis Tate was also due to give an address at the Grand Cinema in the town about 'her recent visit to the German Horror Camps'. The date for this event was announced in the 4 May 1945 edition of the *Somerset Standard* as due to take place on the 13th of that month. By the next week's edition, however, another announcement proclaimed the event as postponed. What had taken place during those seven days was, of course, VE Day. At the end of April 1945, Hitler had committed suicide and he was succeeded by Admiral Dönitz. The latter's leadership was very short-lived though, as a week later, on 7 May 1945, he offered unconditional surrender.

The *Somerset Standard*'s report of that victorious day was as follows:

> The people of Frome and district celebrated V.E. Day with joyous and thankful hearts and an ever-present remembrance of those who have paid the Supreme Sacrifice as a contribution to the victory and those from the district still engaged in fighting the Japanese. Expectancy of the great announcement reached a high tension during Monday afternoon, when the decorating of public buildings and private dwellings was energetically taken in hand. Between intervals of listening to their wireless broadcasts, large numbers of people thronged the streets discussing the possibilities of 'The Day' being declared and even after all doubts had been set at rest by the official pronouncement, there was some 'premature celebration'!

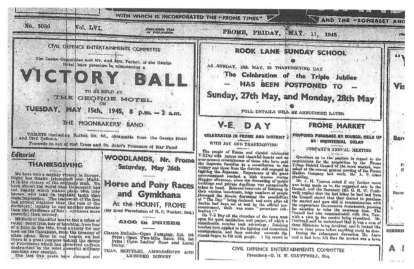

Victory in Europe announced.

On VE Day itself – Tuesday, 8 May 1945 – all Frome churches opened their doors for quiet meditation and prayer, and many locals took the opportunity for reflection on the previous six years or to 'thank God' it was now over. There were also services held in the morning and evening in the churches; one of these, at St John's, being the first united service of the day. It began at 5 o'clock in the evening and was preceded by an hour of victory peals on the church bells; the service itself attracted a 1,000-strong congregation. Later in the evening, the Badcox Lane Baptist Church also attracted a huge crowd of not only Baptists, but members of both non-conformist churches and those from Anglican ones as well.

Earlier in the day, from midday onwards in fact, the streets had begun to fill with people and by the time of the prime minister's historic announcement, a large crowd had gathered in the Market Place to hear it (relayed from a nearby premises). Also, at some time during the afternoon, at least according to the local newspaper report, 'an American soldier in the crowd struck a popular note by playing the British Tommy's famous marching song *Tipperary* on a trumpet.' Celebrations, perhaps not surprisingly, went on into the early hours of the morning, with thousands of people – soldiers and civilians alike – still thronging the streets until then and fireworks being let off around the town. The day ended with church bells still ringing.

A less popular note, however, had been struck earlier in the evening by other Americans. These were Military Policemen – nicknamed 'snowdrops' because of their white helmets – who,

D° 12434

Instrument of Surrender

of

All German armed forces in HOLLAND, in

northwest Germany including all islands,

and in DENMARK

1. The German Command agrees to the surrender of all German armed forces in HOLLAND, in northwest GERMANY including the FRISIAN ISLANDS and HELIGOLAND and all other islands, in SCHLESWIG-HOLSTEIN, and in DENMARK, to the C-in-C 21 Army Group.

   These forces to lay down their arms and to surrender unconditionally.

2. All hostilities on land, on sea, or in the air by German forces in the above areas to cease at 1200 hrs. British Double Summer Time on Saturday 5 May 1945.

3. The German command to carry out at once, and without argument or comment, all further orders that will be issued by the Allied Powers on any subject.

4. Disobedience of orders, or failure to comply with them, will be regarded as a breach of these surrender terms and will be dealt with by the Allied Powers in accordance with the accepted laws and usages of war.

5. This instrument of surrender is independent of, without prejudice to, and will be superseded by any general instrument of surrender imposed by or on behalf of the Allied Powers and applicable to Germany and the German armed forces as a whole.

6. This instrument of surrender is written in English and in German.

   The English version is the authentic text.

7. The decision of the Allied Powers will be final if any doubt or dispute arises as to the meaning of interpretation of the surrender terms.

Friedeburg

Kinzel

Wagner

Pollok

Friedl

The terms of surrender.

according to one local that witnessed the unsavoury episode, took umbrage at the presence of two black American soldiers in the Market Place and began severely beating them; their only 'crime' being that Frome was still an 'alternate' town and, unfortunately for the soldiers, VE Day had fallen on a 'Whites Only' one. However, also in the crowd was a group of British paratroopers; they were recuperating at the Military Hospital at Longleat, but had come over to the town to join in the celebrations. On seeing this blatant act of racism and injustice, the five paratroopers immediately intervened, picked up the MPs and unceremoniously dropped them in the Boyle Cross fountain, much to the cheers and delight of the onlooking crowd.

In the next few days, numerous street parties were hastily arranged and on the following Tuesday, a Victory Ball was held at the George Hotel. The music was to be provided by the Moonrakers' Band according to the announcement for the event, with all proceeds in aid of the Red Cross and St John's Prisoner of War Fund.

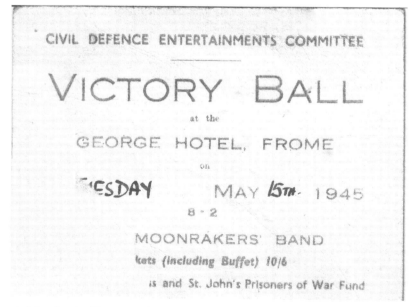

A ticket for the Victory Ball at the George Hotel.

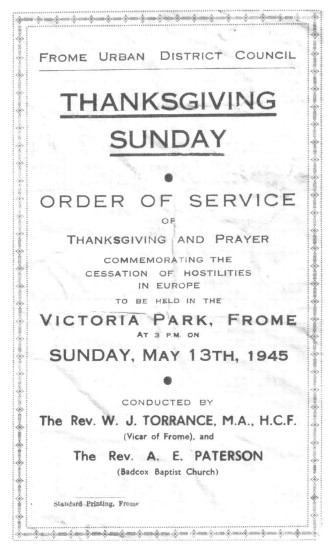

A Victory Thanksgiving Service was held on Sunday, 13 May 1945.

Three months later the crowds were back on the streets of Frome, this time to celebrate VJ Day: victory against the Japanese in the Pacific.

'Although quite a considerable proportion of Frome residents knew nothing of the Prime Minister's announcement at midnight of the Japanese surrender,' reported the *Somerset Standard* after the event, 'obviously quite a number did hear it, for there was considerable jollification in the streets of the town.' Immediately following the announcement, 'parties formed in the streets with drums and all kinds of noise-making instruments, including dust-bin lids and hammers.'

A crowd of around 300 people finally assembled in the Market Place and proceeded up Bath Street to the Police Station, where cheers were given outside it to greet the Union Jack that was promptly hoisted. Fireworks were set off and the spirit of joyous abandonment was very much in evidence, according to newspaper reports, until about 2 o'clock in the morning, when the revellers finally dispersed.

The following evening there was an even greater crowd in the Market Place than had been there for VE Day and instead of the impromptu dancing which had broken out that night, this time music from a loudspeaker on the balcony of the George Hotel lent a more 'organized' feeling to the evening's celebrations.

The people who heard the prime minister's announcement of the Japanese surrender the previous night had listened to it being spoken by Clement Attlee and not the familiar tones of Winston Churchill. This was due to the fact that within the period between the VE and VJ proclamations there had been a General Election in Britain and the Conservatives, led by Churchill, had been well and truly beaten in a landslide victory by the Labour Party. Although Churchill himself did not lose his seat, Mavis Tate, the Frome MP since 1935 did; the ten years of hard work, effort and determination she had put in on behalf of the town seemingly wiped away and forgotten by a single stroke on a ballot paper. Yet the people of Frome, as elsewhere in the country, were building towards a new society. The war was now over, peace was here once again, and the need to rebuild their villages, towns, cities and communities was essential.

Although the war was now over, and despite the Labour Party victory, there would still be reminders of the conflict for

German prisoners of war held at the Bath Road camp.

several years to come. Rationing was no doubt the main one, but anyone travelling along Bath Road until 1948 could not help but notice men in overalls of a distinctly Teutonic nature. These were German prisoners of war, still being held in what was known as the 'White House' work camp, otherwise the Mendip Lodge Hotel. For the most part they undertook farming work and, especially once the war had finished, their situation became much more relaxed. The camp housed, at its peak, around 300 PoWs. During the subsequent war the 'camp' would make the newspapers several times. One of these was due to a prisoner having committed suicide by jumping off the railway bridge at Berkeley. Although at the inquest his fellow PoWs could give no obvious reason behind his action, the suicide victim had, according to one witness, just received letters from home; one from his father, the other from his girlfriend. The witness did not see the contents but perhaps the latter correspondence began 'Dear Hans'. Another newsworthy story concerned an 'escaped' PoW who eloped with the daughter of the person he was helping to paint their house. The third story related to a football team assembled by the PoWs and although only just established, they

Many of the inmates were sent out into the local community to undertake work.

ENTERTAINMENT AT THE P.O.W. CAMP IN FROME

German prisoners were allowed to create their own entertainment.

seemingly beat all-comers, scoring a massive thirty-six goals in only three games against local opponents. Like the evacuees, many of the prisoners stayed in Frome or kept in contact with people there, some even marrying local girls.

For the German PoWs, the war would soon be over and they would return to their homeland, as would the Allied PoWs whose home was Frome. Slowly, all of them, along with the communities to which they returned, would rebuild their lives, mourn their dead and set about creating a better world for themselves and their children; one that did not involve war. A global conflict was never meant to happen again after the first one, but it had. This time around, however, there was now a greater need to make sure that this remained true.

Afterword

Although there are numerous statues and sculptures, panels and plaques, busts and benches, memorials and monuments, as well as other physical reminders of the war such as gravestones, gun emplacements and pill-boxes in and around Frome and the surrounding villages, perhaps the true legacy of its participation in the war can be gauged by the number of get-togethers, reunions, meetings and events which have been organized or spontaneously occurred over the decades that have elapsed since the end of the Second World War. These have brought together many of those who, at the time, went through common experiences, be they evacuees, American GIs, merchant seamen, relocated factory workers or even German prisoners of war.

Over the years these gatherings have included those by the former schoolchildren of Coopers' Company's School, Evans

Naval war veterans, members of the North Russia Club, South West, who served on convoy patrol vessels during the Second World War in the icy waters of the Arctic, attended their 10th anniversary dinner at the Keyford Elms Hotel, Frome. The event was once again organised by Mr Curly Morris. Among the guests were the president of the NRC, Mr Chris Tye, from Chatham. Also in the photograph, left at the back, are four ex-boy seamen who served together in 1941-42: Nobby Clark, from the Isle of Man, Mr Ken Small, Midsomer Norton, Mr Norman Mintern, of Evercreech, and Mr Curly Morris.

Newspaper report on one of the many reunions that took place after the war.

The bench commemorating Coopers' Company's School's wartime stay in the town.

Engineering employees who came up from Portsmouth, and many men who served on the dangerous Arctic convoy runs, along with specially-commissioned events such as Frome Society for Local Studies' 'They Came to Frome'. It is perhaps a mark

FROME URBAN DISTRICT
ROLL OF HONOUR BOOK

Recording all those who served their Country during the 1939–45 World War
ending on August 15th, 1945, who were Residents of Frome on 1st March, 1939

NAME	RANK (at time of compiling records)	UNIT	PERIOD OF SERVICE	NOTES AND REMARKS (including Decorations, Mentions, P.O.W., Killed or died on Service and wounded)

(Please write in BLOCK CAPITALS)

Relatives were asked to send details of loved ones for inclusion in the Roll of Honour.

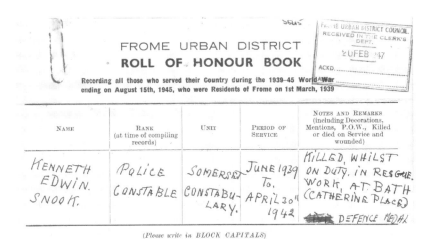

'Roll of Honour' card for Kenneth Snook, who died in April 1942 during the Bath Blitz.

Frome's official War Memorial, outside the Memorial Theatre.

of respect the town of Frome holds in the hearts of many who were not Frome-born that they, or their relatives, pay a visit to the town or surrounding villages year after year. Indeed, the Frome Museum receives many of these visitors, either looking for information or simply just looking.

However, many of these seemingly temporary visitors during the war became more permanent ones after it was over, choosing to stay on and not return to their previous homes. Again this list includes child evacuees, relocated employees and, in at least one case, a former German prisoner of war. Also many of those who stayed on after the conflict did so by marrying local men and women.

If nothing else, the Second World War seems to have been a war of community: vast numbers of people – many at first

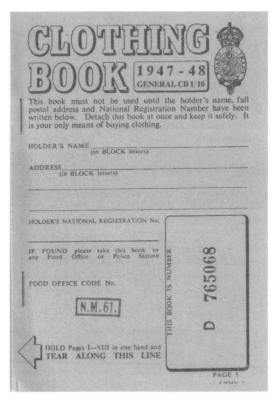

Rationing continued long after the war had come to an end.

D.2016/3

FROME WAR MEMORIAL FUND APPEAL

OME URBAN DISTRICT COUNCIL
CEIVED IN THE CLERK'S
OFFICE

-3 JUL 1948

A.CO. ....
AN.J ....
COPY TO ....

PUBLIC OFFICES,

FROME.

DEAR SIR/MADAM,—

I have the honour upon behalf of the War Memorial Committee to invite your most generous interest and support in subscribing to the provision of a " GARDEN OR REMEMBRANCE " as a Memorial to the men of Frome who gave their lives in the service of their Country 1939 to 1945.

At a recently held Public Meeting the Committee was elected and briefed to obtain £1,000, to ensure that the Memorial could be commenced and completed outright.

This therefore is the sum appealed for, and if each person in Frome plays his or her part the object should be speedily achieved.

May I suggest that this is a debt of honour.

Fifty-eight men of Frome gave their lives that each one of us could remain free to accept, acknowledge and commemorate the ideals for which they died.

This is your opportunity to perpetuate their memory—you surely will not fail them !

Please send donations to WAR MEMORIAL COMMITTEE, PUBLIC OFFICES, or MIDLAND BANK, Frome.

Collecting Boxes, together with photographs of the proposed Memorial, will be placed at convenient centres.   It is not intended to publish the individual amounts subscribed but only subscribers' names.

Yours faithfully,

H. M. SCOTT,
Chairman of Appeal Committee.

Frome War Memorial Fund Appeal.

strangers to each other – who bonded throughout those six years to the degree that the various people they met or the places in which they found themselves – within Frome or the surrounding villages – were never forgotten. Obviously, these gatherings become fewer and perhaps further apart as the span of time between the war years and the present grows ever greater, and those who participated sadly pass on or are no longer able to undertake the journey, but hopefully this book can act as a kind of gathering-place for all those memories. It is hoped that these are accurately portrayed, or else, for those who were not there, serve as a starting-point to learn more about what it was really like to live through *Frome at War 1939–45*.

Roll of Honour

Frome men killed on active service during the Second World War. Names are followed by rank, section of the armed forces, date of death and, where available, age (in brackets) at the time of death:

ARMED SERVICES:

ADAMS, D. R., Gunner, Royal Artillery, 25.11.1939 (20)

ANSTEY, L.J., Second Lieutenant, Royal Berkshire Regiment, 23.05.1940 (21)

ARMSTRONG, G., Guardsman, Coldstream Guards, 16.03.1942 (26)

ASHFORD, H.G., Leading Telegraphist, Royal Navy, 06.05.1942 (32)

BEALE, F.A., Guardsman, Grenadier Guards, 27.09.1944 (27)

BERGIN, J., Bombardier, Royal Artillery, 04.02.1944

BLACKWELL, G.T.W., Lieutenant (Quartermaster), Royal Sussex Regiment, 18.05.1940 (41)

BLAKER, G.B., Major, Hampshire Regiment, 01.07.1944 (25)

BOWER, C.N., Sergeant, Royal Air Force (VR), 24.02.1942 (28)

BREWER, A.A., Ordinary Seaman, Royal Navy, 02.10.1942 (19)

BUCKLEY, H.H., Gunner, Royal Navy, 10.08.1940 (51)

BUNCE, R.S., Sergeant, Royal Air Force (VR), 09.06.1941 (22)

BURFORD, C., Sapper, Royal Engineers, 15.06.1944 (23)

BURGE, L.J., Gunner, Royal Artillery, 30.10.1943 (25)

BURGESS, A.A., Aircraftman, 2nd Class, Royal Air Force, 13.09.1940 (18)

BURGESS, J.P., Private, Border Regiment, 18.03.1945 (28)

CARPENTER, T.E., Petty Officer Stoker, Royal Navy, 28.11.1939 (50)

CARPENTER, W.J., Trooper, Royal Armoured Corps, 28.06.1942 (26)

COLEMAN, F.G., Sergeant, Somerset Light Infantry, 10.07.1944 (32)

COLEMAN, S.F., Sergeant, Royal Air Force (VR), 24.09.1944 (20)

COLES, D., Sergeant Pilot, Royal Air Force (VR), 29.06.1943

COOK, R.J., Flight Sergeant Pilot, Royal Air Force (VR), 08.11.1944 (21)

COTTLE, C.R.F., Cook (S) D/MX, Royal Navy, 10.12.1941 (29)

COURTNEY, M.L., Private, Royal Army Ordnance Corps, 18.06.1941 (20)

DAVAGE, F.A., Trooper, Royal Armoured Corps, 28.05.1944 (21)

DUNFORD, E.R., Flight Sergeant, Royal Air Force (VR), 11.10.1944 (32)

DUNN, F.J.C., Lance Corporal, Royal Engineers, 23.05.1940 (26)

DURNFORD, R.G.G., Lance Bombardier, Royal Artillery, 18.12.1942 (33)

DuVIVIER, R.A.L., Pilot Officer, Royal Air Force (VR), 30.03.1941 (26)

EVANS, T.G., Lieutenant Commander Surgeon, Royal Navy (VR), 05.11.1940 (43)

EVANS, W.G., Private, Pioneer Corps, 05.11.1944 (23)

FRAPWELL, A.W., Sergeant, Royal Air Force (VR), 13.04.1943 (22)

FRICKER, F.W., Private, Royal Army Ordnance Corps, 15.02.1942 (30)

FUTCHER, E.J., Private, Somerset Light Infantry, 03.08.1944

GARNETT, G.F., Signalman, Royal Corps of Signals, 18.08.1943 (23)

GARRETT, W.A., Leading Aircraftman, Royal Air Force (VR), 22.04.1943 (26)

GRANT, J.F., Petty Officer Stoker, Royal Navy, 23.10.1943 (33)

GREEN, A.G., Gunner, Royal Artillery, 19.08.1943 (22)

HEATH, D.G., Corporal, Royal Armoured Corps, 14.11.1942 (22)

HEATH, R.A., Aircraftman 2nd Class, Royal Air Force (VR), 29.11.1943 (33)

HIGGINS, R.C., Private, Royal West Kent Regiment, 23.10.1944 (24)

HILLIER, T., Sergeant, Royal Air Force (VR), 26.11.1943 (24)

HINDE, R.W., Leading Aircraftman, Royal Air Force (VR), 09.12.1941 (20)

HINKS, A.R.J., Private, East Yorkshire Regiment, 06.06.1944 (23)

HIRST, S., Corporal, Seaforth Highlanders, 10.01.1945 (34)

HODDINOTT, J.L., Trooper, Royal Armoured Corps, 30.06.1941

HOLE, J.G., Sergeant, Royal Air Force (VR), 29.06.1943 (21)

HOUSE, W.G., Leading Aircraftman, Royal Air Force (VR), 27.04.1944 (40)

HUGGARD, C.R., Private, Royal Army Ordnance Corps, 03.10.1943 (29)

HUGHES, R., Private, Cornwall Light Infantry, 15.04.1945 (22)

HUMPHRIES, E.J., Private, Suffolk Regiment, 11.06.1944 (33)

HUNTLEY, F.G., Sergeant, Royal Air Force (VR), 07.04.1942 (21)

HURDEN, J.A., Able Seaman, Royal Navy, 14.12.1940 (20)

INMAN, C.H., Sergeant, Royal Army Service Corps, 14.02.1944 (26)

IRISH, J., Ordinary Seaman, Royal Navy, 02.05.1941 (27)

JAMES, C.F., Stoker 2nd Class, Royal Navy, 16.02.1942

KEEVIL, J.J., Sergeant, Royal Artillery, 01.03.1942 (32)

KELLAWAY, H.S., Stoker 1st Class, Royal Navy, 03.05.1941

KELLAWAY, L.R., Able Seaman, Royal Navy, 29.06.1940 (29)

KERSLAKE, W.P., Sergeant, Royal Air Force, 01.12.1942 (24)

KING, C.T., Sergeant, Royal Air Force (VR), 25.12.1943 (23)

KING, M., Sergeant, Somerset Light Infantry, 10.07.1944 (26)

KNAPTON, C.F., Aircraftman 2nd Class, Royal Air Force (VR), 06.12.1940 (25)

LAMBTON, J., Flying Officer, Royal Air Force (VR), 11.08.1941

LAY, E.D., Gunner, Royal Artillery, 23.04.1945 (19)

LEE, M.A.W., Sergeant Pilot, Royal Air Force (VR), 31.12.1940 (21)

LEE, W.G., Trooper, Royal Armoured Corps, 12.07.1943 (32)

LEWIS, G.M.K., Sapper, Royal Engineers, 03.10.1940 (21)

LIFELY, R.A., Trooper, Royal Armoured Corps, 11.06.1944 (23)

LUCEY, E.J.M., Sergeant, Royal Air Force, 06.05.1941 (28)

LUKINS, E.C., Private, Wiltshire Regiment, 04.09.1940 (21)

LUKINS, W.I.R., Driver, Royal Engineers, 01.03.1944 (27)

MARKEY, A.W.J., Mechanician, Royal Navy, 10.12.1941 (41)

MARKEY, S.G., Private, Somerset Light Infantry, 12.05.1944 (27)

MILLARD, R.W., Corporal, Royal Engineers, 27.06.1944 (32)

MILLETT, A.L., Stoker 2nd Class, Royal Navy, 24.02.1941

MILLS, W.J., Sergeant, Royal Air Force (VR), 25.06.1942 (27)

MOON, G.A., Lieutenant, South Wales Borderers, 27.01.1944 (29)

MOON, R.E., Private, Australian Infantry, 13.08.1944 (37)

MORGAN, E.W., Pilot Officer, Royal Air Force, 02.07.1944 (26)

NEWLYN, A.A.E.J., Stoker 1st Class, Royal Navy, 08.06.1940 (24)

OLIVER, F.J., Petty Officer Stoker, Royal Navy, 16.06.1942 (29)

OSBOURNE, R.D., Flight Sergeant, Royal Air Force, 19.08.1943 (32)

PAGETT, R.F., Driver, Royal Army Service Corps, 25.06.1946 (27)

PALMER, R.F., Leading Seaman, Royal Navy, 15.03.1942 (22)

PARADISE, G., Sergeant, Royal Air Force, 02.11.1944 (33)

PARKER, H.J., Pilot Officer, Royal Air Force, 31.07.1942 (27)

PARKER, R.E., Leading Aircraftman, Royal Air Force (VR), 16.04.1946 (24)

PATCH, J.W., Petty Officer Pilot, Royal Navy, 18.04.1945

PEARCE, F.A., Corporal, Royal Marines, 26.12.1944 (55)

PEMBER, R.C.G., Captain, Scots Guards, 29.03.1945 (24)

PERKINS, D.J., Sergeant, Royal Air Force, 31.12.1944 (21)

PHEAR, C.T., Guardsman, Coldstream Guards, 06.11.1943 (28)

POOLE, G.F., Leading Aircraftman, Royal Air Force (VR), 07.11.1944 (33)

POPE, W.A., Trooper, Royal Armoured Corps, 27.06.1944 (20)

POTHECARY, F.W., Marine, Royal Marines, 15.10.1941

RITCHINGS, J.D., Bombardier, Royal Artillery, 18.05.1946 (27)

RUMBLE, C.H., Leading Aircraftman, Royal Air Force (VR), 31.12.1944 (20)

SEVIOUR, D.H., Stoker 1st Class, Royal Navy, 15.12.1941

SHARPE, H.G., Sergeant, Royal Air Force (VR), 12.05.1941 (29)

SHAW, W.H., Guardsman, Coldstream Guards, 18.06.1944 (21)

SHAWE, J.C., Lieutenant, Royal Artillery, 22.05.1940 (23)

SMITH, E.G., Private, Somerset Light Infantry, 10.03.1944 (20)

SMITH, R.W., Corporal, Royal Corps of Signals, 08.09.1946 (24)

SMITH, W.D., Private, Somerset Light Infantry, 12.02.1945 (29)

STARR, J.R., Sergeant, Royal Air Force (VR), 21.01.1944 (21)

STOATE, E.L., Trooper, Royal Armoured Corps, 29.08.1944 (29)

TABER, A.J.A.J., Sergeant, Royal Armoured Corps, 10.12.1940 (24)

TAYLOR, R.W., Sergeant, Royal Air Force, 28.06.1942

TAYLOR, W., Private, Somerset Light Infantry, 10.07.1944 (26)

THICK, A., Leading Stoker, Royal Navy, 12.11.1942

TUCKER, J., Private, Royal Army Medical Corps, 17.09.1944 (25)

TURK, H.S., Private, Somerset Light Infantry, 02.10.1944 (24)

TURNER, A.J., Marine, Royal Marines, 17.07.1943 (19)

VINCE, D.A., Sapper, Royal Engineers, 18.08.1940 (23)

WALTERS, W.D.A., Private, Royal Army Ordnance Corps, 15.04.1941 (25)

WEEKS, K.J., Ordinary Seaman, Royal Navy, 17.01.1942 (22)

WHATLEY, E.A., Sapper, Royal Engineers, 11.11.1943 (37)

WHITEFIELD, K.W., Flight Lieutenant, Royal Air Force (VR), 11.11.1944

WILDEN, R.F., Flying Officer (Pilot), Royal Air Force (VR), 13.06.1944 (22)

WILLIAMS, C., Private, Somerset Light Infantry, 27.09.1944 (29)

WOODLAND, G.K.S., Sapper, Royal Engineers, 26.06.1945 (19)

CIVIL DEFENCE:

BARNES, E.G.C., Warden, ARP, 12.04.1941 (62)

COLE, W., Warden, ARP, 15.04.1941 (56)

PRICE, G.C., Volunteer Home Guard, 03.04.1941

SNOOK, K.E., Constable, Somerset Constabulary, 26.04.1942 (25)

(VR) = Volunteer Reserve

Bibliography

Primary Sources:

Adams, D., *Frome's Fallen Heroes of World War Two* (Adams Publishing, 2008)

Arthur, M., *Symbol of Courage* (London, Pan Macmillan, 2005)

Belham, P., *The Making of Frome* (Frome Society for Local Studies, second edition, 1985)

Berryman, D., *Wiltshire Airfields in the Second World War* (Countryside Books, 2002)

____ *Somerset Airfields in the Second World War* (Countryside Books, 2006)

Brown, D., *Somerset v Hitler* (Countryside Books, 1999)

Brown, M., *Evacuees* (Sutton Publishing, 2000)

Curtis, J. (ed.), *Frome Victoria Hospital 1901–2008* (Victoria Hospital, 2008)

Davis, M. and Pitt, V., *Historic Inns of Frome* (Akeman Press, 2015)

Delaforce, P., *The Fighting Wessex Wyverns* (Sutton Publishing, 2002)

Dike, J., *Bristol Blitz Diary* (Bristol, Redcliffe Press, 1982)

Disney, F., *Shepton Mallet Prison: 403 Years of Prison Regimes* (Francis Disney, 1992)

Emden, R. van, *The Last Fighting Tommy* (Bloomsbury Publishing, 2009)

Falconer, D. and Falconer, J., *Bath at War* (Sutton Publishing, 1999)

Falconer, D. and Falconer, J., *Bath at War: The Home Front* (Sutton Publishing, 2001)

Farmer, A., *Teach Yourself: The Second World War* (Hodder Arnold, 2004)

Gardner, E., *A Somerset Airman* (Steyning, Red'n'Ritten, 2005)

Gardner, J., *Wartime Britain 1939–1945* (Headline Books Publishing, 2004)

Gill, D., *Frome School Days* (Frome 1300 Publications, 1985)

Goodall, R., *The Buildings of Frome* (Frome Society for Local Study, second edition, 2005)

Hawkins, Mac, *Somerset at War* (Wimborne, Dovecote, 1988)

Hebditch, F., *Somerset in the Second World War* (Somerset Books, 2005)

Hersey, L. and Mason, C., *The West Country at War* (Broadcast Books, 1995)

Hill, D., *Bath Fire Brigade and Ambulance Service 1891–1974* (Millstream Books, 2003)

Inglis, R., *The Children's War* (London, Collins, 1989)

Lassman, D., *Frome in the Great War* (Pen & Sword, 2016)

MacLeay, A. and McGarvie, M., *Frome Society Year Book* (Vols 1–21), (Frome Society for Local Study, 1987–2018)

McGarvie, M., *Frome Through The Ages: AD1000–1999* (Somerset Standard, 1999)

Payne, John (ed.), *Home in Frome: Working Memories* (Millstream Books, 2012)

Penny, J., *Bristol at War* (Derby, Derby Books Publishing, 2010)

Perry, G.S. (ed.), *The Coopers' Company's School in Frome 1939–1945* (G.S. Perry, 2006)

Rothnie, N., *The Bombing of Bath* (Monkton Farleigh, Folly Books, 2010)

Smith, G., *When Jim Crow Met John Bull* (I.B.Tauris & Co. Ltd, 1987)

Somerset Women's Institutes, *What Did You Do In The War Grandma?* (Countryside Books, 2005)

Vivian-Neal, A., *Roll of Honour of County of Somerset 1939–1945* (Taunton, Somerset County Memorial Fund, 1949)

Wilson, J., *The Somerset Home Guard* (Bath, Millstream Books, 2004)

Wray, T., *The Somerset Underground: A History of the GHQ Auxiliary Units in Somerset 1940–1944* (Mirador Publishing, 2016)

Newspapers:

Bath Chronicle

Somerset Standard

Somerset and Wiltshire Journal

(All permissions for photographs not in the author's or Frome Museum's collections have been sought wherever possible.)

Index